To ~~Steve~~, TI is ezaut...
~~see~~ and u
respected ;
easier to i
May you f.....
this book that bring you Joy and
inspire you to relive memorable
experiences!

Stel DM...
JAN 16, 2015

DISCOVERING

YOUR

TREASURES

Inspirational Prose

STEPHEN McDONALD

"QUOTES"

"When the memories flood your mind, there is a lot right and nothing wrong with you...the reasons are known yet unspoken, because they are too special to share with others"...

"Was it not for my thoughts I would have nothing to drive me. Was it not for my abilities I would have no way to act on my thoughts. Was it not for my judgment I would have no way to evaluate my thoughts. Was it not for my conscience I would have no way to control what I think. Was it not for my faith I would have few reasons to hope and without hope I have no reason to think in the first place"...

"I climb mountains because I have the will to take that first step. I walk miles because I take the initiative to prove that I can. I have a great feeling in my heart because I dare to take the time to do for others. I am who I am because I refuse to settle for what others feel that I should be...so don't dare to think I am weak"...

"MAKING LIFE A MEMORABLE ADVENTURE"

No one can write your true life story for there are so many bridges that you have crossed in your lifetime that even you have forgotten some of them. Each bridge represented a challenge for you. Although others may have watched or even crossed them with you, they don't know the true significance crossing those bridges had on your life.

In life, making choices is often our greatest challenge, for it brings change to our lives. One must understand how life is to be lived to understand the significance of embracing change and the memorable adventures you will have with you forevermore. I consider success as being one's most significant change in a lifetime, for we are all born with only the will to live. Through change we acquire all of our skills, knowledge, character, feelings and yes, our personal net worth.

I define success as "one advancing his/her family name at least one generation". Why, well as a general rule if you don't help then you are hurting the effort. You cannot do this if you don't embrace life based on what I call "The Five Elements of Living"...Faith & Religion, Family, Friendship & Love, Inspiration and Fun.

This book is very different in that it is a collection of one page mini-themes based on my experiences in life and my thoughts about how these five elements enrich living. I did not set out to write a book, but it happened and that is a true example of change and how it leads you to memorable adventures. I hope you enjoy reading it because I really enjoy expressing my thoughts to those I meet each day of my life for that is how I know how well I am living life...

August 30, 2010

"WITH MY PEN I WRITE"

Long ago, before I knew I had it in me...I thought like I felt all others thought. I discovered later in life that I could speak what others wanted to hear...I am religious so I am spiritual...and I am educated, but more importantly...I am wise for life has taught me much. So now "with my pen I write" for me...to release that which is within me. I pray others will understand me and for others to learn what I know...in hopes that one day they too can say "with my pen I write"...

For what good is a dream unfulfilled...a house not lived in...a boat not sailed...a storm not on shore...a shoe not worn or a path not traveled? What use is a tool in the shed when you need it now...a rock when you need a knife... a rope when you need a pole...a wrong step when an issue is pressing or loving one that does not want to love you back? "With my pen I write" in hopes that when read by others, my words will help them on their journeys through life...

"With my pen I write" about what God has allowed me to learn...what life has taught me...and what living life has presented me. So much of my life's journey is in every letter I put on a page. .every phrase my mind composes and every writing that I pen. "With my pen I write" for my writing can be preserved forevermore...therefore, preserving the legacy of my life as I rest in eternity with my Lord, my God...

September 20, 2008

CONTENTS

FAITH AND RELIGION

"For those moments when life seems to have conquered the greater part of you, find hope in knowing that some parts of you are still refusing to be conquered"...

"A MORNING LIKE NO OTHER"

How can you explain Christmas and not understand the blessing from Heaven given to man? Christmas is "a morning like no other"...

Things like the importance of tomorrow, the battles that rage on today and even the men who dictate what others must do, all respect Christmas day, making it "a morning like no other"...

A child sleeps at night, but this night sleep is filled with excitement...for tomorrow is a special day. You see Santa Claus will visit tonight. How can you share the excitement of a child on Christmas morning...and not know it is "a morning like no other"...

Be it white with snow, or sunny and hot, should a storm bring rain with a rainbow too, should you wake with pain or feel your best, the constant is...that Christmas morning is "a morning like no other"...

Christmas morning is "a morning like no other", for no other morning can bring joy to so many, hope to those in despair and comfort for those threatened. Families are once again united, love is everywhere, battles cease, combatants get a day of peace and tears flow freely in households everywhere. But mostly, Christ is remembered...yes it is "a morning like no other"...

December 21, 2008

"A TIME LIKE NO OTHER"

A calming feeling just came over me. I believe it is "a time like no other"...

A timely blessing was just bestowed upon me. I believe it is a" time like no other"...

The sun is shining with clouds all around it...I believe it is "a time like no other"...

In a wilderness where I have not journeyed, I have found my way. I believe it is "a time like no other"...

In troubling times and situations, I have peace of mind. I believe it is "a time like no other"...

I believe it is "a time like no other", because at no other time have I been so blessed and so at peace...this is "a time like no other"...

December 19, 2007

"BLESSED"

Yesterday, as I worked to improve me, there were others that tried to stand in my way...

Yesterday, when I worked hard to gain and keep my faith, others kept telling me that God was not the way...

Yesterday, as I saw others in need and offered or gave a helping hand, others stood looking but helped no one...

Yesterday, love came to me and stayed a while, only to fade away, while others just took love for granted...

Now here I am often alone, trying to do my best. Others look and some like what they see, while others look away in search of more, something different that requires less than their best. That's not me...

I hope one day that they understand how they are "blessed" to be alive, to make their own choices and to accept only that which they desire. "Blessed" that God provides it all, gives them life and protects them well. "Blessed" we are, for God is real...

October 25, 2007

"CHRISTMAS WISH"

I wish you peace of mind, for it is a gift you must give yourself...

I wish you joy, for joy allows you to give from your heart...

I wish you hope, for hope gives you the desire to be and the desire to keep living...

I wish that your faith is strong, for faith allows you to act as you must...

I wish that you possess love, for love gives you a reason to live...

I wish that God is your Savior, for He will always deliver you and bring comfort to your soul...

Give from the heart that which no one else can give, to allow you to receive what is given to you.

How wonderful life is, when you are blessed with faith, hope, joy, peace and mostly love...

MERRY CHRISTMAS!

December 19, 2009

"GOD IS MY BURDEN BEARER"

The first prayers I heard I did not understand, for I did not know of God. I did not know anything but how to cling to mom and cry when I was not happy. I grew, I learned and I discovered me...and that allowed me to discover God. In Church I learned that "God is my burden bearer"...

The old song tells us that troubles don't last always. Murphy's Law warns that things will go wrong. Life has proven both theories are true. Man I am glad I am saved and that I am blessed for "God is my burden bearer"...

When troubles come into my life I can choose to deal with them in the way that I feel is right. The minor ones, I have the knowledge and strength to overcome on my own, but the major ones take so much more. The Bible teaches that one should pray and bring your burdens to God. I am so excited to testify that "God is my burden bearer"...

Here I stand in the valley of sin with the devil's evilness all around me. I see no apparent path to take, no beacons to guide me and no stars or the sun to light my way. So, I close my eyes and pray. Lord I need you...and you know why. I faithfully come to you, for I know you will bring me joy. I hope others understand your power and how compassionate you are. I know my path to eternity will be walked with thee, for "God is my burden bearer". Lord, God, my burdens...I bring faithfully to thee...

December 24, 2008

"I NEVER FAILED TO PRAY"

Life was not my choice...and I thank my parents for giving it to me. My gratitude is shown by how I live my life. Those I respect and love have always shown and taught me how to live life. My yesterdays have passed and each day I can say "I never failed to pray"...

A seat was all she wanted. Fame was not in the plan. Most stand to make a point, but Miss Parks sat down and made her point; a point that helped to change the history of our land. Once she was free again, her actions had made her known by many. I am certain that if asked, she would say "I never failed to pray"..

Wisdom comes with age as does so much more. Like it or not there is a price to pay for living your life. The price has not changed, for today we all will pay the same price that Adam and Eve paid. The price for living is dying...and it will never change. Understanding this is why "I never failed to pray"...

Prayer has always inspired me to dream and live those dreams. Prayer always delivers me when I know not how to overcome despair. Prayer has always comforted me when fear tried to destroy my joy. Prayer has always moved me in the right way when hope was needed the most. Heaven is full of those that can say "I never failed to pray"...

August 15, 2009

"I'M NOT PROTECTED, I'M BLESSED"

When standing on the hillside with an army behind him, the little lad David was faced with a great challenge issued by the giant, standing so boldly in the valley below. With fear in their eyes, they all watched, as he marched just as boldly to meet the challenger below. No weapons of war he carried, for he had not proven them. Only his slingshot and three stones he carried into battle, for he had faith that God would deliver him. Standing victoriously after slaying the giant...he thought, "I'm not protected, I'm blessed"...

Apollo 13 and its crew of three set off to do what man had never done before. Thoroughly trained they were for the mission as planned. When something went wrong, it appeared they were doomed never to get home, but God had His own plan. Through transmissions with man on earth, the miracle happened and they splashed down in the ocean as others before them had. Each of them had to have thought, "I'm not protected, I'm blessed"...

When trouble is upon you and there appears to be no way out...and you think you just cannot win...it is then that prayer should be your plan...as your weapon in the battle, your ship in the water, your ledge on the side of the mountain, your air bag in a crash...or the mender of your heart or your healing portion. "I'm not protected, I'm blessed" for God is always with me...I feel Him right now...

May 10, 2009

"MY BOAT NEEDS NO ANCHOR"

I feel the way the world turns and know it can get stormy. I know in days to come...fierce winds will be blowing to make my boat an unsafe place to be. I fear not troubling times for they cannot harm me...for my boat is a great one...

My boat is built by the master Craftsman and the plans have no flaws. The tools He uses are forgiving and the materials will last for an eternity. His helpers all have halos and are faithful always. The sounds of their labor are joyous music to all. I have no complaints for my boat is a beauty...

It is never totally finished, yet it is always ready for the open waters. There are many other boats like it, for the master Craftsman is never too busy to build you a boat of your own. There is no need to pay Him...if we love each other and put nothing else above Him. I will keep living by His doctrine, that captain Moses received from Him...as written on the stone tables...

You may think my boat, which is a beauty, should have an anchor upon it... but no anchor you will see. You see "my boat needs no anchor" for it is always moored in God's harbor. Even in treacherous or stormy waters, I don't fear... for my journey is always safe. Have Him build you one and you too can say "my boat needs no anchor"...

March 01, 2009

"MY TOLL IS CHEAP, MY SOUL IS INVALUABLE"

Waking in the morning from a restful sleep is so normal that I take it as a given. No my friends, it is a blessing...and my only toll is to say thank you Lord...

That peaceful sleep was made possible by this comfort zone I am in. I have shelter, nourishment, safety, security and mostly my faith that God would care for me through the night. My only toll is to say...thank you Lord for letting me see another day...

I understand that "my toll is cheap, my soul is invaluable" because having faith in God is a choice with no consequences. Having hope for tomorrow is uplifting and not costly. Being joyous is only refreshing and kind words are only spoken treasures from the soul. Know that helping others takes a little bit more because your soul becomes more invaluable...

I understand why "my toll is cheap, my soul is invaluable" for my Lord, my God allows me to live and he loves me more each day. My toll is to love others as he loves me. My Lord provides for me and my toll is to help others in need. My Lord shelters me from danger so my toll is to testify for him. My Lord made my soul invaluable; my toll is to keep it that way...

You see my brothers, "my toll is cheap, my soul is invaluable". My Lord, my God... I am yours for now, tomorrow and forevermore...so use me as you will for "my toll is cheap, my soul is invaluable"...

September 21, 2008

"SOME STORIES NEVER GET OLD"

Poems, songs, as well as good books, have a story to tell. You need only to listen as you read or hear them to understand their true meaning and get a glimpse of the author's soul. No, not all are appealing to you and some you never even finish. Yet there is always one or more that touches your soul. Isn't it amazing how "some stories never get old"...

"Some stories never get old" because of how they touch your soul, how they bring you to that peaceful state of mind, how they comfort you when you need it the most or how they replace your sorrows with exciting dreams of how tomorrow can be. I imagine that even in Heaven the Angels sometimes sing...of how "some stories never get old"...

One of the best stories is of how Christmas began...for who cannot appreciate this story of Christ. From the Immaculate Conception to the faith of Joseph...to the leaping of John just to be close to Him even before He was born. Just consider His deliverance from the king...and the gifts from the wise men...They all show the greatness of God. Because He was born in a manger for there was not room at the inn...I celebrate this day each and every year for "some stories never get old", especially the story about the Savior of our souls...

November 30, 2010

"STANDING ON THE SHOULDERS OF MANY"

To achieve you must first desire what you want to achieve, whereas to win you must first start what it takes to win...

Most of what you will ever do has been dreamed, desired and at least attempted before. That is why benchmarks exist for you to exceed, for you to raise the bar, set a new record, be the first to conquer or achieve...

We are always coached that you should stay focused on the goals and work to move forward...forget your failures of yesterday and never look behind you. This is good advice that always helps you to achieve...

Now that you know the positive way to think...it is good for you to know where you stand. We are all "standing on the shoulders of many"...we need only to look toward Heaven to visualize how far we must go...

Be sure you are standing on the right shoulders, for you must have faith that the shoulders will support you. You must have hope that the shoulders are supported by greater shoulders below. You must trust that the shoulders will support you as you reach faithfully for your dreams...

The price for "standing on the shoulders of many" is being prepared to have others stand on your shoulders...when they are needing to dream first, then achieve greatness, to become shoulders for others that dare to dream, to stand on...

November 08, 2008

"THE BOX IS ONLY PART OF THE GIFT"

We may not be expecting a gift that is given, but a gift always lifts our spirits. The excitement of seeing it, then removing the wrapping makes our hearts beat faster and faster until the eyes behold the gift. The gift then dictates our following emotions...and hopefully, within...you know that "the box is only part of the gift" for someone cares enough to have given it...

Just imagine how the giver thought of you...then thought of how to find just that right gift for you! Then think of how the giver...unselfishly chose the perfect wrapping for your gift! Visualize the giver taking the time to make sure each fold of the wrapping was...just perfect! Can you see the love that went into tying the bow...and writing those special words on the card? Believe me when I say "the box is only part of the gift" so savor the moment forevermore...

When I open my gift I want the giver to be there...so I can watch their excitement grow in concert with mine. I want to see the sparkle in their eyes...when I validate that they chose the perfect gift for me. I want to feel their heart beating just as fast as mine...when I hug or kiss them to show how I feel. I want the giver to know that I know "the box is only part of the gift" ...for knowing that they care means so much more...

December 16, 2010

"THE CROSSES I BEAR"

The first cross of significance is the cross that Jesus carried for all of us. It is so amazing how that cross became a symbol of all that was to become. Yes someone else carried the cross for Jesus, for he was carrying a greater burden than anyone else would ever know or experience. I can hear Jesus saying "the crosses I bear" bring salvation to all that believe in me...

Some look at me and wonder why I am as they see me. Many will never understand me for they know not what is in my soul. Life gives us all chances to prove our net worth to the world. Some take the easy or popular way and others know their purpose and assume the role of bearing crosses for others. "The crosses I bear" are my commitments to Christ and a token of my appreciation for Him dying on the cross for you and me...

Are there crosses that you could bear for another? Should your life end today, can you rest in peace knowing you helped those which could not bear their crosses alone? Do you understand that you cannot always bear your crosses all by yourself? Mostly, do you know that Christ is always there should the burden of your crosses be too much for you? I do, so "the crosses I bear" includes crosses that others cannot bear alone...for I know Christ will always help me carry my own...

June 30, 2010

"THE FOCUS IS STILL ON THE CHILD"

I don't know how you came to know of Christmas or how you feel about us being reduced to saying "Happy Holidays". I don't understand how we have allowed our focus to be blurred so much that we have to think twice about saying "Merry Christmas". It has been 2010 years and man is still better off if "the focus is still on the child"...

The wise men were focused on finding him for it was the demand of their king. The star came to sparkle over him for it felt too much joy to keep it within. The rest of him being born was all God's doing. God planned it so that the wise men would go another way so that the Believer would know that "the focus is still on the child"...

As gifts are chosen and given or received there is a constant that we all share. "The focus is still on the child" within each of us, the child that never grows too old to believe. Yes "the focus is still on the child" whose birth gave us the key to the kingdom and whose crucifixion gave us salvation. So even tomorrow if "the focus is still on the child", the soul is on the path to eternity...

December 15, 2010

"TOMORROW WILL COME"

Now there are events that most of us will never hope for and pray that we never attend. Life is lived each day in hope of seeing tomorrow. We spend time with those we love and share such memories as we create together. When I am alone...the memories are still with me. When you are alone...those same memories I hope you have of me. "Tomorrow will come" with or without me, so cherish the memories you have of me...

No, there is no good time for a loved one to leave us and it will always be hard to cope with. Faith and hope will help us face each coming day and we must prepare to live our life...for "tomorrow will come" and we know you would want us to live happily, sharing memories of having you in our lives...

"Tomorrow will come" and there will be many tomorrows afterward...and the constant challenges of life will always be with us. The uncertainty of when each of us will join you in Heaven...we will never know. What is certain is that we will miss you and relive each memory of you that we have...each day of our lives. Those memories will have to do...until we are reunited with you as Angels in Heaven...

March 26, 2010

Stephen McDonald

"WHEN I AM TROUBLED, I FEEL YOUR STRENGTH WITHIN"

Many days I have worked to keep the lives of others safe. I often put my life on the line at times. Through hails of bullets, slashing blades of death, fierce right crosses and deadly kicks, I trusted in thee. Lord "when I am troubled, I feel your strength within" and hope gives me strength to carry on...

We all need some pleasure to balance what work demands of us. I love to enjoy all the beauty that you created just for man to care for. As I walk through the wilderness...I know there is some danger near me even if I don't see or hear it. "When I am troubled, I feel your strength within" and my fears are overcome by my faith...that you are walking with me...

When I am sleeping, it is because I feel it. When I awake each day, I feel it. When I feed myself, I know why and I feel it. With each step I take, I know there is another safe step to make, all because I feel it. I hope you see why "when I am troubled, I feel your strength within" and move faithfully through life trusting that you will always be my burden bearer...

November 1, 2009

12

FAMILY AND FRIENDS

"You should always cherish the person that brings you peace of mind"...

"All that you understand about life is useless if you do not understand the situation you are currently in"...

"A DAUGHTER'S THOUGHTS"

When she looks at me...I know what I hope she sees. For as long as I have lived, she has been my strength...so I hope she sees the strength in me...

When she talks with me...I know what I hope she hears. She taught me my first words and now...I hope I speak as strongly as she...

When she is silent or sleeps...I know what I hope she thinks. I have her faith and desire to live...so I hope she thinks I'm a survivor too...

Mom, my mom...you mean so much to me. More than I can speak...more than eyes can see. Only our hearts truly understand...what will forever be a mystery for others to solve. For only a daughter can walk in the steps of her mom...and know what her mom means to her...

October 14, 2006

"A FATHER'S FOOTPRINTS"

Even as a child you wanted to be like him, even if you did not know why or understand what you were doing. His shoes you would put on your little feet. Your legs could barely lift them so you just shuffled around. You would fall and stand to try again. Those shoes left a lot of footprints. You see, "a father's footprints" should show you the way...

Father left for work each day, leaving you home to play. Oh, how you played each day pretending you were at work...just like you knew your father was. Years passed and to school you would go...and when asked, you proudly told how your father went to work each day. Remember how excited you got when he came home each day? "A father's footprints" should always lead you, even if you don't know it...

Life is not this way for all ...for many never know their fathers...and they may not even carry their father's name. Many live in fear...for their fathers are not

real men. Many live in shame...feeling that their fathers are not worth knowing. They all cry out in varying ways...for how can they learn and live with no
true path to follow. "A father's footprints" are missing and the child is left to
find their own way...

"A father's footprints" are not always there for you to follow...and sometimes
they show the path not to take. Sometimes not being able to see them...is the
best thing for you. Fortunately, there are always "a father's footprints" to follow...for God's footprints are always there. Follow His footprints and your
children...will have "a father's footprints" to follow...

January 4, 2009

"A LAUGH OR A SMILE"

When others think of you, I really don't know their thoughts. I just hope that
they share mine. For the morning is highlighted by the energy that you always
seem to have. The day never passes when we don't hear your voice command-
ing respect, yet in such a respectful way. "A laugh or a smile" is what we have
grown to expect each and every time that we see you...

The pressures of the job, we know how they can come down on each of us.
The voice of the boss is always demanding more in less time and oh, make sure
it is correct! It takes courage to face such challenges and more courage to bear
the burden that is always there. With "a laugh or a smile" you just keep march-
ing on, so determined and so inspiring to those around you...

Life has it way of revealing one's true strength as it does one's true character.
We want not to be judgmental, but how hard is it not to be impressed when
someone blows you away with their courage, passion for life and unwavering
energy and drive to achieve. "A laugh or a smile" matters not to me for I know
in both there is sincerity...

October 10, 2011

"AT LAST I SEE THE LIGHT"

As a boy, there was a lot that I did not know or understand. Some things, oh they were so hard to learn and some even harder to do...

"Life is simple at your age" the adults would say, while I agonized over what I did not know or understand...

"Keep growing and study hard" they would always say, especially when I wanted only to play...

Time, you know it does not stand still, so I grew, I learned and I even understood so much more...

Then one day I heard me say "son, life is simple at your age. Grow and study hard and it will pay off one day"...

His look reminded me of me back then...and I realized the lights are now on in me, "at last I see the Light"...is drawing him to me...

August 28, 2007

"A LITTLE WOMAN WHO STANDS TALL"

What is dear to me I protect constantly and always. What I love, I always fight to keep. What I fear losing, I hold on to more tightly to let no one or nothing take it from me. I can be defined as "a little woman who stands tall" just watch me to know why...

God gave me many tools to use so I can get through life. It is on me to know which ones to use and how to use them well. It is my duty to not waste any of the blessings that God gives me daily. Daily, I work to improve myself as well as those around me. I'm "a little woman who stands tall" and while I achieve I also give of the blessings that God has given me...

The biggest are not always the best and the smallest are not always weaker. Education is only great if you have the common sense to use it appropriately. Now wisdom, I truly have earned and there is nothing better when you blend it with your blessings from God. That is the secret to why I am "a little woman who stands tall". Now...help me bring more joy to us all...

October 30, 2010

"AS MUCH AS I GIVE, IT IS ONLY PART OF MY TREASURES"

Now that you have experienced the person that I am and have found comfort in the way I give, I need to explain something that most don't know. "As much as I give, it is only part of my treasures" within ...

You need only to listen to my voice to be rewarded with pureness that can only come from a loving soul. You need only to experience the sensitivity of my touch to know that beneath my skin are veins of precious love that originate from my heart. I truly know that "as much as I give, it is only part of my treasures" for only I know of all of the treasures to be found within me...

Look into my eyes to find the entry to the treasures within me. Now just imagine all of the great memories which have entered as you just did. Can you see their images or relive them with me? Can you tell the ones that mean the most to me? Have you yet recognized that they are all treasures that no one else can cherish? Now, do you understand as I do that "as much as I give, it is only part of my treasures" for I can never give more to others...than the treasures that God keeps giving to me...

August 30, 2010

"BABY BRO, GIVE THE WORLD THE BEST YOU GOT"

I tried to project myself inside of your mind, not to control it but just to understand. There is an iron curtain that protects your soul, your way of keeping others a safe distance away. The secret code is there somewhere for us to find so we must keep trying. "Baby bro, give the world the best you got" we will be there to help you protect your treasures...

We know of some of your treasures for you have given us a few glimpses before. We know of your character for we share the same name. We know you are spiritual for God chose you to preach the Word. We know that you are gifted, Lord knows you can "sang". "Baby bro, give the world the best you got" share what God has given you while uplifting His name...

Something is troubling you that is plain to see. The Devil has not bested you for God's Angels are protecting you, preserving your treasures while God bears each of your burdens. You may see life as a valley of despair and your burdens as giants in the likeness of Goliath. Just have no fear for we have faith in thee...

Your voice is your slingshot and God will provide the stones, the messages He gives you. Stand steady, make ready and "Baby bro, give the world the best you got" for your treasures are gifts which will strengthen you as you bring hope to others in God's name...

September 18, 2010

"BE HIM TO NEVER LOSE HIM"

To fully appreciate the better things in life you have to remember some of the worst adventures that have occurred in your life. Time has a way of reminding you of those bad adventures just when you need to appreciate something life is giving you today. Dad would tell us that "You are rich and don't know it". I understand that so much better now and have learned to "be him to never lose him" or my memories of being with him...

If I can give as he gave, it will bring joy to my soul. If I can bring the smiles to others faces as I watched him do so often, oh, a joyful laugh all will have. If my emotions let others know the purity of my heart as his emotions always did, then others will know it is okay to show they are emotional too. I know now that I must "be him to never lose him" in my lifetime...

When you think of a great father or man, there will be common characteristics that you will appreciate so much. When you spend time with such men, experiencing the wisdom that they can share, you may be overwhelmed, but you will never stop thirsting for the knowledge you know is there. If I "be him to never lose him" hopefully one day someone will honor me in the same way...

June 17, 2011

"BEING A MAN IS AN ETERNAL JOURNEY"

A child is born and it is a son. One day son...you'll be a man. We take that to be a fact, but hold on one minute it is not as simple as that. "Being a man is an eternal journey"...

The days will pass and son you will grow. The ways of the world, one day you will know. It's training day every day so son...make sure that you learn what you must become in life. Learn that education is not free…and that many challenges await thee. "Being a man is an eternal journey" …one that no one else can make for thee…

As an adult, you should have accomplished much…but all is for naught if you don't learn to be a man. It is not an automatic status given to those in their late teens. It is a status you earn…son. Money, fame and fathering a child do not make you a man. Your character, your actions and maturity means more. Son, please understand that "being a man is an eternal journey" that always requires your best …

Study the character of real men…then take actions to be like them. Don't just grow…mature more each day. Watch the people around you for they will let you know…if you are a real man or just a grown up son. Mostly listen to your conscience and feel with your heart…for it is then you will know, that "being a man is an eternal journey"…one that you must travel for the rest of your life…

December 14, 2008

"BRIDGING TIME"

There is a flowing memory that I constantly dream of…a memory that brings me joy and gives me hope for a better tomorrow. That memory is always "bridging time" from my yesterday to what I dream my tomorrow will bring…

I enjoy seeing me as a child again…laughing and playing without the cares that I constantly face currently. I see me as a young child…so ready to experience the life that I constantly dream of. Even my thoughts back then were "bridging time" from innocence to maturity…

My desires are my proof that I am constantly "bridging time" for with each new thought I always start with yesterday and find the faith to hope for a tomorrow that brings me that which I dreamed today. If you see your birthday as an annual opportunity to recognize that you are "bridging time", time will reward you with dreams built on your most joyous memories of yesterday…

August 17, 2011

"BROTHER MICHAEL"

In the winter of one's life...one hopes only to see summer again. In the darkest hour of one's night...one visualizes often just seeing light again. In the bottom of one's deepest pit...one hopes only for the way out...

In one's most joyous moment, one wills one's self to make it last forever. When one has hope and faith...one conquers what challenges him. With what God and His angles provide...one's path through life is paved...and one needs only to walk it to glory...

"Brother Michael", you faced the death angel while walking that path. He landed a deadly blow that shook you much. Down you were and the doctors counted you out...

Know for certain that God is the only Counter that matters...so you celebrate with us, day after day... smiling as your footsteps keep appearing on that path God has built just for you. We love you my "Brother Michael", so live on, live long...and walk your path to eternity...

May 31, 2008

"BROTHER SHERMAN-APRON MAN"

My nose is under attack and the battle it faces just keeps on going...it is raging and yet my nose just feels no pain...it keeps on taking what attacks it and appears to enjoy it...

My lips are beginning to make those smacking little moves...yes, in anticipation of what they hope to encounter...enjoy...it is a good sign for my stomach which awaits more nourishment...

Now it is on my tongue...that taste, that taste sends messages to my brain... my brain knows what was coming to be for the nose and the lips had delivered a warning before...before that taste was known by the tip of the tongue...it fills the mouth now and happiness shows in my eyes...

That cook with the apron on...he is not just a cook, no...he is one heck of a man...a man with it all and he loves to use his skills to please us all. He makes sure that all that eat...are all satisfied, full and when asked only says...that meal was almighty good... "Brother Sherman-apron man"...

July 4, 2008

"BROTHER...REMEMBER WHEN"

Love that lasts through the best or worst of times...the memories we shared will always be mine. Just think back and share with me...for they are rare like great wine...

"Brother...remember when"... life was simple so we played most of the time. We never had to think too much or plan our day...and we received cheers for our accomplishments. We laughed at each other's actions...while mom and dad made sure we did not lose our way...

"Brother...remember when"...we learned to be responsible, learned to protect and care for each other too. Side by side fighting for our place in life... and hoping to live forevermore. It was those years, those times that helped us to be great brothers....and we should not forget those days, no, no, not ever...

We are now grown with children of our own, homes, cars and so much more that some are unknown. Those memories are now mixed with those... life has brought our way...so, so many that sometimes we know not what to say...

So "brother...remember when"...let's live it again and again, until our journey on earth ends. Promise you will...until the last one of us is gone home. Then in Heaven I will ask you again..."brother...remember when"?...

June 29, 2008

"BUILD A BETTER ROAD TO TRAVEL"

If you stand still for a moment and reflect on your past, you will have many thoughts to think about. The answer of how you got to where you are will be there for you to discover. The joys and pains of your life until this moment will be remembered too. If you are happy with what you see, it will validate how good of a road you have traveled. If you are not happy with what you see, "build a better road to travel" for you owe it to yourself...

Start with a plan based on faith that God will always walk with you. Have faith that your tomorrow will bring greater joy and less pain...and that what you built yesterday prepares you to build today...the road you must travel tomorrow. "Build a better road to travel"...for tomorrow you must journey on...

Build it with a solid foundation of hope and understanding...so you will be able to find enough peace to finish the surface that you must travel. For without hope...the desire to try just will not be there. Without understanding, you will not be able to build your road correctly...leaving pitfalls and deception to block your path. "Build a better road to travel"...for others closest to you may need to follow it too...

Now it is time to build a surface...knowing that it is all that others will ever see. The surface must contain compassion, love and joy...if others are to be drawn to it too. Go on now, kneel down on your knees...for only prayer can mix the components to build your road. If you feel the hands of God as they guide the Angels that are helping you...just ask for forgiveness and pray for strength...to be able to "build a better road to travel"...

Then with each step you take on each tomorrow...give thanks that you had the strength and faith to become a better person. That person who will "build a better road to travel"...a road that others will want to travel with you. For at that last moment of your life, when you remember the road you traveled...there will be no time to "build a better road to travel"...

March 14, 2010

"DADDY'S LOVE IS NOT JUST WORDS"

He paces as he waits on your arrival. Not just for your birth...but always. Always hoping and praying for your safety, success and happiness. You should know that "Daddy's love is not just words"...it is seen in the endless steps he has paced while waiting to know you are well...

He was so patient when teaching you to ride your first bike....so did you notice the pride when you did your first solo ride? He admired your strength and courage when you met life's challenges day after day...so did you feel his presence supporting your every action? He is so good at helping that you hardly notice he is there...because "Daddy's love is not just words"...

There is no need to fear or no reason to ever doubt it's there...for there are so many times that it is proven to children everywhere. Be it wiping a tear from one's eye, encouraging you to give it one more try, or even that occasion when his feelings are expressed by saying..."I love you". It is comforting to know that "Daddy's love is not just words"...it is all that he gives and everything that he does...

June 12, 2010

"FATHER, CAN YOU HEAR MY TEARS"

From the first time you saw me, I know you loved me and promised God you would always care for me...

From the first time you held me, I knew your strength and could feel your love for me. When you saw my first tears, you comforted me by wiping those tears away...

I grew and I learned to live, falling often along the way. Even when you were not there with me...the distance did not keep you from comforting me. "Father, can you hear my tears"...is that why I am always comforted when I think of you...

I am all grown up and facing all the challenges that life presents me... for I am living by the values mom and you taught me. I am feeling my way through the gauntlet of choices available to me. I am making my life and living it well...and I have many stories to tell those I love. As I conquer my fears and rise from my battles with despair...I often wonder, "Father, can you hear my tears"...

"Father, can you hear my tears" of joy or my tears cried mostly when my heart ached. What about my tears of sorrow...when I lost what I loved or was distanced from them that I wanted? "Father, can you hear my tears"... If you can, then let me live for me...and live my way. For even if others are in my life...you know I am yours always. Our bond is strong because we both know...that you and only you...can hear my tears...

October 18, 2008

"FATHER'S IMAGE DEFINES MINE"

The world and those you know are the mirrors that should mean the most... for one can always justify their own image that is looking back at them. Mirrors don't reach out to you or question your actions...they are only your visible reflection. Hopefully you feel like me...for I know that my "father's image defines mine"...

All that you have acquired or learned is of little importance...if the image the world sees leaves haunting memories. Without respecting others...how can you expect respect in return? When your album of life includes only images of you...it is obvious that your image is not in the albums of others. My "father's image defines mine"...so my album of life is filled with images that reflect...how others cherish me...

Father, you are a great image to me...an image I share with so many more. You are not known for heroic deeds, but to me...the little deeds you do mean so much more. I try each day to define me in a way that...the image in the mirror honors thee. I join the world in knowing my "father's image defines mine"...and I hope one day that my image inspires my child to say..."father's image defines mine"...

June 6, 2010

"FOREVER YOU ARE MINE"

For nine months I carried you...so "forever you are mine". In time you will make me proud... and for now you give me joy...no, you are the joy of my life...

Inside of me you became something, something created because of love... from an egg you became my child that was born. I remember the first time I held you in my arms and I said to myself..."forever you are mine"...

Very little you were back then...and day by day you grow, grow to be a bigger bundle of joy. You love your toys, that all can see...while inside I know how much you love me. I am happy to face tomorrow for I know..."forever you are mine"...

In years to come there are days I hope to remember, that first attempt to crawl then...you will walk. Yes you will fall, just to rise again. Oh how proud I will be each time you do well. I will be prouder then, proud of your strength, proud of your dreaming and proud of your accomplishments. Yes I pray you will be just like me and more importantly..."forever you are mine"...

March 20, 2009

Stephen McDonald

"FRIEND"

For a lifetime, I did not know you...for yesterday I had not met you...and except for a chance meeting...I never would have met you...

For a little while I spoke to you. When the conversation became comfortable...I spoke with you. It was only a few minutes...but then how long does it really take...to think of one as a friend?...

Friend, the relationship is young...but the hope of a better friendship is just as close as our next conversation. Let's be friends... even if, we never meet again...

November 19, 2008

"HIS SHADOW GROWS WITH EACH STEP I TAKE"

As a small child I played day after day not knowing my future...and not knowing to care that I didn't know. I was laughing most of the time and trying new things. Some of which caused me to cry...when my father would discipline me. It was like he was everywhere! It appears to me that "His shadow grows with each step I take"...

As a teen, life started meaning more to me. I could understand my father's role in my life. He provided for us, kept us safe...and showed us love in so many ways. I now understood why it was like he was everywhere. I was beginning to understand why "his shadow grows with each step I take"...

In college I discovered what it was going to take to be the man I had become. I understood father's teachings, why he disciplined me...and why his strength was so often displayed with just that look he had. Yes...even in his silence. As a man I now know why "his shadow grows with each step I take"...

With a family of my own...my father's shadow is still always there. I now know it shows me the path to success...and how to live life right. It directs my focus in those times...when I don't know what to do. It points out my strengths...when the battles are raging around me. It shades me...when the heat of living threatens to burn my joy away. So each day I am comforted by knowing...that "his shadow grows with each step I take". Daily I pray that my children feel that...my shadow grows with each step they take...

June 7, 2009

28

"HOME IS FOREVER IN MY HEART"

I had a life to live as a child...and I thank God that my family was with me each step of the way to care for me and show me love. I was encouraged and I was challenged by my family to be successful...to be the best that I can be. I am of age now so I must enter the world. I am ready for...I know "home is forever in my heart" so I move on faithfully...

There will be differences and challenges that I have not known before. I know change is necessary if I am to be a successful adult. I know the challenges will be many and some...I may fail to meet. Yet I have confidence that each tomorrow will find me closer to my goals...and I will be stronger too. "Home is forever in my heart" so I will succeed always...by finding the strength within me...

What home has always meant to me is my secret weapon...that the world will soon learn to respect. Home has that greater power we call love...and no distance or circumstances can tear it from my heart. When I think of home...joy returns to me. When others elect to put their trust in something different...I will remain as I am. For "home is forever in my heart"...and life for me will be highlighted forevermore...by the love I have for home ...

June 13, 2010

"HOME OR JUST A HOUSE"

I wake and know just where I am...I see familiar things, hear familiar sounds... I feel like I belong here where I am...I stretch, I moan, I know it is time to start my day...I rise and remember how Pop would say "rise and shine, your troubles aren't mine"...for a moment I go back down memory lane, because those thoughts anchor me to my childhood...

I think about the good and bad and all the fun that I had...I think, I laugh, sometimes I even cry tears of joy. I feel my youthfulness and know that it is what gives me my adult strength. I always come back to reality and start my day...and I know that at the end of this moment of reminiscing...this is just a house...it is not my home...

June 20, 2007

"HOW TO THANK AN ANGEL"

Every life is a God given gift that only one person can live. God uses each person in a unique way to bring joy to others, comfort and care for them too. You may not realize all that you do for others, yet you know how it makes you feel when others are a reflection of you. We, your family, are caring, sensitive, loving and giving for we know "how to thank an Angel"...

Your wisdom is founded in your faith in God. Yes, you have always been a loyal and unselfish sister, wife, mother and grandmother to us all. Our paths may have been walked a little differently from yours, but we always knew we never walked those paths alone for you were always there guiding our lives or showing us the way to live life. Each day we grow closer to you for we all are walking our paths knowing too that God is our savior. Because of you, we are learning "how to thank an Angel" and live unselfishly...

Others should let your sweetness and friendly character guide them as it has guided us. They should take note of your feisty approach to living through trying times. They should tap into your wisdom so they too can be caring, loving and faithful while giving freely from the heart. Then they too will know "how to thank an Angel"...

You are a great role model for you used the gifts God gave you in that unique and special way. You kept wealth and riches as well as fame and popularity in their proper place behind God, family and living faithfully. You even gave us all your greatest gift of knowing "how to thank an Angel". Now we believe... we can be Angels too...

August 6, 2010

"HOW WILLING AM I"

Sometimes I just cannot be all that my soul drives me to be. I have a great desire to give to those around me...and I have an inner magnet that cannot be seen, only felt by those I touch. "How willing am I"...just listen to others and there...your answer will be found...

People, people come be with me...come enjoy life enriched by kindness, honesty and love that is hard to find. From a distance it can be felt...but up close it is lived. Breathe in the happy air around me... for that air gives me all that you see. "How willing am I"...just ask the stars and they will twinkle to let you know what they think of me...

It is not hard to be around me...for I bring so much that most need. No drama...no pain...so there is no shame in my game. "How willing am I"...in time you will know as others do...that I am always willing to help...yes it is true...

August 7, 2009

"IF I STUMBLE, DON'T LET ME FALL"

Brag all that you want, say what you please, but know that is not strength...to that I just say, man please...please look around you to behold nature...now that is real strength...

Politicians, yes they control a lot...while promising you this just to give you that. They paint you a pretty picture then...give you only a sketch. They pound on the podium demanding you choose their names...but what they don't know is that God blesses me with all that I need...

Strength is not always power you know...for often it may be a teardrop or a gentle touch. Strength only becomes strength when it proves to be. My strength is in me...being who and what I am...

Lord "if I stumble, don't let me fall"...help me stand to journey on. The life I have is all mine...even if it is not so perfect in many ways. It is not joyous all the time...for it is often clouded with disappointments, hurts and lots of pain. Still, I am so proud when they call my name....I am Carolyn Jean and if you know me you know what I stand for...

I stand for God and that will never change. I stand before Him with a family that does the same. A family with whom I share a name...so brothers and sister I say it with no shame. "If I stumble, don't let me fall" for if you stumble...I stand ready as always to hold you steady...

October 26, 2008

"I'M THE DOUBLE NICKEL AND GOING STRONG"

One day back then, I could not imagine...what I know now. I could not visualize...what are now yesterday's memories to me. I could not feel comfortable with life...as my faith and wisdom now allows me to be. Now days some tease me, but that is okay. "I'm the double nickel and going strong" keep pace with me if you can...

I am now the one looking over the top of my glasses...giving those stares that I once dreaded. I talk so boldly about that which I know...while the young ones wonder how I automatically know the answer. I smile when issues are presented to me...for my wisdom tells me I must help the young learn. Mostly, I listen patiently...for that is how others know I care. "I'm the double nickel and going strong"...God, please don't call me home...

Life seems to go faster with each passing year...and you cannot stop or even slow down...no matter how hard you try. "I'm the double nickel and going strong"...come sit with me to gain wisdom of your own. Come see the excitement...that you must live to possess. Come enjoy...my comforting touch. Come listen to some old war stories...of what life has given me. You must live your young life...preparing for the faster living to come...

You must embrace the dreams of your journeys of tomorrow...so when you live long enough to say "I'm the double nickel and going strong"...you will be able to increase your pace of living as each year brings more challenges your way. Each conquest is an adventure that brings you wisdom and strength to journey on. It is through sharing and giving of that which you have...that you can clearly see how to live faster...faster than you ever have...

January 30, 2011

"LET ME LIVE FOR ME"

Beyond the skin that you see...is the person that is me. Through these eyes I see the world around me...and behind these eyes is all that I am. Whispered words don't hurt me none...so I answer silently, "let me live for me" because I let you...live for thee...

I know me better than you ever will. So understand that in knowing me...I know what matters most to me. If you don't understand me, it does not mean there is nothing to know. The right person I will let in...and let know all of me. For the rest of you...just "let me live for me" for I like living peacefully...

Frustration is a way of life and none escapes it. We all must deal with it and it is how you deal with it that makes you feel as you do. It makes you frustrated...if you let it be so. Now love me or hate me, it is your choice...but changing me is only on me. I let you...so "let me live for me". I ask that you just support me...constantly...

Help me, my Angel; I need to see the way. Lord help me to pray and help me be...better each day. Give me strength to live with me and deal with all others that are looking for a way in. Lord strengthen me...when my patience grow thin. Then comfort my soul...so I can stay in control. Bring peace to me to understand this life I live and teach me the right way...to give joyously of me. Lord, please guide all others so that they will "let me live for me"...for I live my life faithfully...for thee...

February 19, 2009

"LORD, IF IT IS MINE"

Inside I know what I have gained and what I have lost. Joyous moments are forever recorded in my memories. My younger years I lived in a loving home... a home that I know will always be mine. "Lord, if it is mine"...allow me to relive the memories each day...and to share them with those I love...

I look into my little one's eyes and he looks up at me...I know he looks up to me too. This brings joy to my soul and some comfort for the pain I know I will always feel. "Lord, if it is mine" to feel forever...then always let the joyous memories bring me comfort day after day...

As I help those in need and help to educate those thirsting for knowledge, may I continue showing those that know me...that strength is gained in how great of deeds one does. That joy will come to you...even with painful memories that never go away. "Lord, if it is mine"...let others see how well I live on...

Lord, if this cross you have given me to bear is the test of my faith in Thee... If it is how I must show how much you mean to me...or if it allows me to bring joy to those that I see...then "Lord, if it is mine"...bless me with many years and give me the strength to bear it...always letting others know that they too can have joy in the midst of their pains, by bearing their cross just as I do...

November 22, 2008

"MY CUP OF COFFEE"

Many drink it for that morning "pick-me-up"; some drink it to stay awake. Some drink it because others do and some drink it because it is the trendy thing these days...

For me "my cup of coffee" is so much more. It takes me down memory lane to a place and time I love to relive day after day, my childhood. Yes, it started for me at age two with my brother, my closest friend and I, sitting at the table having a cup with our dad. It seldom gets any more special than that...

Now, it was not just a cup of coffee, it was my cup filled with coffee. Probably more milk than coffee back then, but most importantly, it was coffee made by and served with my mother's love. A memory worth remembering forevermore...

"My cup of coffee" has changed throughout the years. I drink that which is made by others now. Some say it is a habit, I know it satisfies a secret passion I have which pleases me. It is when I drink that cup that I make myself...that satisfies that passion and gives me more...

In "my cup of coffee" is the strength...my dad passed on to me. That love and comfort...that only mom can give...and that camaraderie and closeness... that only a brother can be. Each time I drink a cup, I am blessed by God in knowing... I have enjoyed all that we shared in years past. "My cup of coffee" is a reflection of my life and how I came to be...the person you know and see...

August 24, 2008

"MY FAMILY IS MY LIFE"

I was born all by myself, but I was never alone. Mom was always there, before others could see me and all the way to the end. Dad was there too, like God meant for it to be and hard times did not drive him away...

Together they were a great team, real parents, providers, teachers, mentors and yes, my dearest friends. The challenges were daily and many for they had a big family, boys, girls, family and friends. The type of family that would fight with you to the very end...

Time has a way of making you grow old, but the rewards are great if you just trust in the Lord. Now as an adult all that I learned as a family member keeps me sane in a world where few have any shame...

Greatness is achieved by being great and the value of your life is measured by how you live your life. My family is my inheritance in this life time, so don't ever try to short change me. "My family is my life" and they mean everything to me...

June 20, 2007

"MY GREATEST GIFT"

Life is as simple as you make it for in the end it is who and what you are that matters the most. Wealth and fame are great to have and often they come because of the way you live...

The first wealth you obtain is the love for others, the trust they have in thee, the respect you have earned and the kindness you are known to show. This is wealth that the economy can't affect. Only your way of living makes it change. Your heart is the vault that keeps it safe. The withdrawals and deposits are controlled by your teller, Mr. Conscience...

Your name is the gift given to you; a gift from your parents. A gift you pass on to your children. Your fame is not measured by your performance on a stage, instead it is measured by the love and respect others have for you, by the excitement they have just for being with you and by the memories they cherish and hope to obtain when tomorrow comes...

I watch you and I like what I see. I hope and I pray, then I work on me. For I know if I can become what I see...the man you are...I will be wealthy and have fame in my vault too. "My greatest gift" to all, is to one day be thought of just like thee...Grandpa...

December 20, 2008

"MY SECOND PROMISE IS"

As I grew, I knew of the world I lived in and learned more about it with each passing day. When the time was here for me to show greatness...others tried to overshadow me. I was sold by those I loved, for they feared me...not knowing that in years to come I would be the only one...that could protect them. I am Joseph and "my second promise is"...to always be faithful to God and protect those I love...

I was anointed king by those believing in me, but first I had to earn the trust of my King which I did...only to be deceived and outcast by my king. He hunted me with a great desire to kill me. When I had my chances to kill him first...I did not. I am David and "my second promise is"...to be the king that all the people believe me to be...as I lead and protect them well...

There will never be another like me...for I lived, helped all and I taught all of God. For envy I was crucified by man and as promised...after three days I rose to assume the power my God granted me. I am Jesus Christ and "my second promise is"...to prepare a place for you in the Kingdom of Heaven...where I am waiting for thee...

My child, I taught you and watched you become the person I can always be proud of. You always expected me to be there for you and I always have been. Now tomorrow is not promised any of us and I know I prepared you to face it...without me. "My second promise is"...to watch over you from Heaven and allow you to feel my presence as you live your life. Always have hope, love as I did, be caring, understanding...and never lose faith in God or yourself. For one day I know you too will say "my second promise is"...

March 21, 2010

"NEVER FORGET YOU CAN LEAN ON ME"

Strength, they say it comes in numbers...or is visible in the size of something, especially man. I'm not saying that they are wrong and I never will...just understand that I have my own measuring stick. You see all of life's challenges are not seen or heard...yet those involved know them well. No one can see one's fallen sprit or truly explore...the depth of one's despair. My brother, just "never forget you can lean on me"...

Once each year we are the same age, distant twins I think we are. When we were very young you taught me so much, yet most things we learned together. Double trouble I am sure mom sometimes thought we were...you the tough one and me the sentimental schemer. Through it all I knew you would protect me and when I was troubled...you would silently say "never forget you can lean on me"...

We are considered middle agers now and our yesterdays are highlighted by shared events...and many separate paths each of us has traveled. Not as mischievous as we used to be, yet we have more pride...and we are as strong as we ever have been. Life has challenged us and we know many more await us. We have no desire to challenge the strength of the other...for there are so many that need us both. Strength and compassion make us a balanced duo. So today, in concert, we say to the rest of our family..."never forget you can lean on me" for I will always be there for you...

February 13, 2010

"NO TIME FOR SORROW"

A sadness I must feel for you meant so much to me. There is "no time for sorrow" for I must become what I knew you to be. A life is lived with much to learn from those you love. I learned so much from you...so I have "no time for sorrow" for you will always be within me...

When my hand is touched by another, I will remember the sensitivity of your touch...and the comfort of your hugs and I will recall all of the moments I shared with you. There is "no time for sorrow" for others need me...to provide them comfort in a similar sensitive way...

When I am face to face with others and I notice the compassion in their eyes...it will bring back memories of the compassion you always showed me. It is then that I can become more compassionate too. I must gain the strength to do just that, so I have "no time for sorrow"...I must live to give the best of me...

I have grieved as I should...so now I must become more like you lived. I must love as you taught me to...and I must grow stronger as well. I must remember how important I am to those that love me...and I must live a great life to be thought of as you always will be. I have "no time for sorrow" for sorrow will rob me...of my most treasured memories that loving you has given me...

February 27, 2010

"NOT ALL GIANTS ARE BIG"

What I carry within me, only I know. What drives me can only be controlled by me. What you see of me is my gift to thee. Believe it or not but, "not all giants are big"...

I was born just like you. I grew and learned and I acquired wisdom too...and all of that helps me to survive along side of you. Can you not recognize what you see when you study me? Don't be blinded, for "not all giants are big"...

I have a comforting smile that allows me to get close to you...words spoken so calmly, that the birds quietly envy each melody. Charming, some say that I am...but it's just another great quality that so few possess like me. Hopefully you know, "not all giants are big"...

I often conquer my enemies without weapons...as I always comfort those that are close to me. I walk through the dangerous world and many don't know how I survive...but I do. "Not all giants are big", but what they do...just may be surprising to you...

August 9, 2009

"OUR BORROWED ANGEL"

To some, you are just a woman that they may or may not see as they pass you by. To some, you have been a beacon of hope for so many years. To some, their lives are so inter weaved with yours that they don't know life without you. To some, you are what they dream to someday be. To me, you are "our borrowed Angel" from God almighty...

Take those that don't know you, give them a chance and it will not take them long to learn of your treasures...treasures that we work so hard to preserve with you. They will feel the warmth that is...more precious than any fire is capable of creating. They will experience that spirit that...has never been broken. They will see the steely way that you bond your soul to those you love. Yeah, "our borrowed Angel" is so very special to this family...

Fear not tomorrow for we will be there with you each step of the way. Hang not onto yesterday's memories for we will live better memories with you on each tomorrow. Sing not the songs of days gone by...for new lyric will come to you as you dream of each tomorrow. No, don't give the unknown much thought...for together we will face each new day and conquer any challenges as we always have..."Our borrowed Angel"...may God bless us with you for many more days to come...

April 26, 2011

"PASSING TIME, KNOW YOU ARE NOT ALONE"

I don't know but I imagine everyday that you wake...you are hoping the miracle will happen today...and if you don't you should be. For it is through hope that we develop the will to try. Only when we try do we achieve...so if you are just "passing time, know you are not alone" for others are watching you...

Your mother wakes each morning...praying that you made it through another night...this is after she cried herself to sleep sometime during the night. Boy this has aged her enough for us to tell...so don't be guilty of just "passing time, know you are not alone" for your mother...is just passing time too...

Your father is a strong man so his will to succeed...is far greater than those obstacles standing in his way...He has conquered many of them while standing ready to meet the coming challenges. Though he does not cry himself to sleep...he too has aged since you were put away. When you are "passing time, know you are not alone" for your father misses you too...

Somehow your pain escapes your soul through your body...it floats on the air of despair to pass through the cell bars and through the prison entrance...to mix with the freedom air. It mounts a cloud to ascend above the air of deceit...crossing the land below, being guided by your vision of the family you love...the family that loves you too. It knocks on your parents' conscience...then creeps in through the cracks of the damaged doors to their hearts...here it lingers making them live the nightmare...over and over again. So it is not just you "passing time, know you are not alone"...the rest of us are praying for you...and waiting for you to come home...

November 19, 2008

"SEVEN STANDING, ONE IN MOM'S ARMS"

This old world never stops turning and time will never stand still. We are born and we grow then we learn and we love and sometimes...we cry and we laugh for that's just living...

Earl and Mattie were blessed with eight of us, all healthy, all good, all full of life. Great lessons on living they taught us well...from the oldest to the youngest...the same stories of living they did tell. We grew to be men and women, being respected by many...but all blessed to be the children of Earl and Mattie...and all happy to be children in Christ that have faith in God. Mom and Dad were called home some years back...leaving the eight of us to journey on our own. They taught us to be inseparable and today...we still are. Sure we have our differences just as others do...yet we stand together forevermore...

Just yesterday Brother Joe was called home too...leaving us with a message of hope forevermore. He said he was tired and wanted to rest...I know not what happened...but this I do believe...Mom extended her hand from Heaven...just to welcome him in...so for now there is "seven standing, one in Mom's arms"...

We seven will be working for the Lord...and fighting on that battlefield just lifting up His name in praise. We will be teaching our children what they taught us...and that which we learned for...some day we seven will be called home too...where we will be reunited in Heaven, a complete family again. I can hear Pop singing loud and clear "When I shall stand on the golden shores I'll be satisfied then". We are now "seven standing, one in Mom's arms" all serving the Lord...and uplifting the McDonald name...

September 27, 2008

"SO PRECIOUS AND ALWAYS SO REAL"

To understand the importance of anything one must study it and spend some time with it to assess its true value. We never value things exactly the same so it is always necessary to accept what you value while allowing others to value what they choose. We truly value those things which are "so precious and always so real" because they bring us peace of mind...

The greatness of the value is dependent on the peace of mind that we have. Think of all that brings you joy and peace of mind and you will be reminded of that special person in your life, Mom. She taught you to love by giving you life and then showing unconditional love to so many. She taught you to care by always being there for her family. She taught you to learn by sharing her wisdom with those willing to listen. Just think about how she is "so precious and always so real" and feel how peaceful you become...

There is no substitute for what a Mom can give or do. You need only to look around you to understand this. She is the basic foundation of the home, the first teacher each of us have known and the one we miss the most when we feel so alone. Mom is "so precious and always so real" so make her gifts your treasures and honor her by being precious and real for as long as you live...

May 5, 2011

"THE CORD WAS CUT, BUT IT IS ALWAYS THERE"

Doctors help and make child bearing a science. Some try to perfect it, but will never do that. God's way is better, for He meant for children to be born. You see, mothers give birth, be it a daughter or a son and that's the way we are all born. At birth, "the cord was cut, but it is always there"...for, your mother...she will always be...

We grow up and have lives of our own...we are spreading our wings to discover what we can become. The relationship with mother may not always be the best...but there is always a relationship with mom. You see, "the cord was cut, but it is always there" for your mother always cares...

Always love your mother...for she will always love you. Know that love flows from heart to heart and hope is everlasting. You will find that joy is a feeling and memories don't require a physical connector to be cherished. "The cord was cut, but it is always there" for you and your mother are connected forevermore...

I love you mom and always will...for you gave me life. Even though the cord was cut, I know it will always be there...binding our hearts together. It may be transparent to others...but the mother and child always know...it is there...

May 3, 2009

"THE DEPTH OF MY SOUL"

If I watch the sunrise, a part of me grows for the greatness of God is there for me to see. If I watch the sunset, a part of me is at peace for God has given me another day. I don't know "the depth of my soul" but I know I am preparing it for eternity in Heaven...

There are hands all around me, hand that reach out to me for something others need. If I put a little bread in the hands of the hungry, then put clothing on the backs of the naked and just touch the hands of the dishearten and give them some of my strength, all will be better and my soul grows deeper. When I remember to pray for the unfortunate, God remembers me as well. Even with all that I give, I truly feel "the depth of my soul" is not revealed...

"The depth of my soul" is growing every day. I have the opportunity to receive more depth with everything that I do. If I can bring joy to others; wipe a tear from an eye; help someone find their way or give my gift of forgiveness. If I am faithful each and every day, there will be hope for a better tomorrow. If I walk the path God reveals to me, "the depth of my soul" will remain bottomless for as long as I live...

October 28, 2011

"THE MAN WE ALL SEE"

From the beginning there have been eyes watching me...some just wanted to care for me...while some were curious about me...and then some wanted me to look back at them...so they could study me. As a youth it did not matter that much to me...but I now know it is about "the man we all see"...

Most think of strength and leadership when they seek to measure me...for wealth and power is the barometer many of you use to assess my value to thee. These qualities are also important when I look at me...but deeper inside there is so much more...I want all of you to know when observing "the man we all see"...

I have a soul filled with love and compassion...and eyes that display my joy... see that smile that leaves no doubt about my integrity. You will hear a voice that's trusting...yes, it is my bond of honesty...then there is my giving heart that helps and comforts...for I have faith that God will always comfort me. "The man we all see"...I hope is pleasing to thee...

"The man we all see"...you ask what drives him to be...and what keeps him trying to be "the man we all see"? The collection of all you see...is founded in the soul that is me. So the next time you think of me...know that "the man you see" is a reflection of...the love within me...

June 6, 2010

"THE NEXT TIME I SEE YOU"

We all are sad this day for the Lord has taken you away from us. You are gone home to rest from your years of labor, years of joy...and even the years of tears. "The next time I see you" there will be tears of joy...tears shed in heaven...

We saw the way our father loved and he walked the road of life with endless joy. He walked the path his father walked...then our father left footsteps too... the path for us to walk. "The next time I see you"...we will be walking those heavenly streets paved with gold and his footsteps will still be...showing us the way...

We knew our mother's touch so well...so tender so right. She cared for us and others endlessly...day after day...as she touched the souls of many with her many kind deeds. "The next time I see you" I will be touching our mother's hand as she leads me too...into the Promised Land...for Heaven awaits me too...

Goodbye my brother...goodbye for now! Goodbye my brother until "the next time I see you"...when God calls me home...

September 26, 2008

"THE VOICE THAT CALLS ME HOME"

When I knew of nothing and could do nothing but develop...it was the voice I heard often and came to know and love. The day I was born I was no longer within that voice...I was a voice for I was now a child with a voice of my own. I knew my mother's voice would always be..."the voice that calls me home"...

I knew little at first and only reacted to what is natural for a baby, but I knew my mother's voice...and it was always comforting me. As I grew and learned to live...I began to understand life. Through all my adventures of living I always remembered and waited to hear "the voice that calls me home". Mother was always the best...at calling my name...

Life has tested me and given me all that I dared to earn or accomplish. Mother's voice was always in my mind, yes it has always been...a great part of me. Oh how I hope my mom is God's chosen Angel that delivers me the last message that I receive on Earth...for I want her voice to be..."the voice that calls me home"...

April 30, 2010

"THERE ARE NO PERFECT FRIENDS"

If we could control our thoughts and our anger...oh how wonderful life could be. If we could control our emotions and be forever compassionate...oh how loved we would be. Since that is not very realistic...you must understand, "there are no perfect friends"...

Different we are and that makes each of us unique...like it or not that is the way it is. What we want from others is usually a reflection of what we want to be. It is something that each of us long for inside. Let your soul feast on your thoughts and quench its desire to be pure...for you too must keep trying...for "there are no perfect friends"...

You should be more understanding of what others need and want of thee... for they have to do the same for you. Let your heart make you more desirable... by being what others desire...also let your love be measured...by the love you are given...and let your life be defined...by those lives that merge with yours. You should never forget that "there are no perfect friends"...for you too will be defined as...the friend others believe you to be...

December 20, 2009

"THERE IS THIS MAN"

As a child I came to know him and throughout life "there is this man" that has always been special and unique. He taught me a way to live life and always was there to pick me up when I had fallen or lost my way. He helped to heal my many wounds, yes even my broken heart. Through him I became me, so I hope I am as special to him as he is to me...

Within me "there is this man" that is a constant reminder of how I must always strive to be. For compassion, love and respect are just a few of my character traits that he helped me develop for me. I would not be as knowledgeable or strong as I am, had I not learned from him that I had to work to satisfy others and me. You see, "there is this man" within me that I carry always as the image I truly hope to be. There is a need, so I gladly share him with my community...

In the future, "there is this man" that will always be with me. Helping to comfort and protect me. Through my memories of life with him, I will always have his strength and become more joyous as I think of him. Dad, "there is this man" that I know and it is you. I pledge to love you always for I know that it is your love for us, that has made me know that "there is this man" around, within and in my future forevermore...

September 3, 2011

"THIS CUP I DRINK FROM"

Life brings you challenges which you must acknowledge first...and then work at overcoming. What is one person's sorrow...is often another person's joy. "This cup I drink from" is from God and I know it is filled with blessings for only me. I pray that you know...that you have a cup of your own...

I have lived my life which only I can live...with those I love and those that love me. I have something that is desired by no one for it attempts to destroy my body at times. I have lived with it and will continue to live on...for it is a blessing just like all of the good ones. "This cup I drink from" doesn't always contain greatness...for there must be bitterness for one to savor the sweetest of God's blessings...

When the pain comes...I realize I am blessed to be alive and have many around me that love me. I can still see the beauty around me...and feel God's comforting hand touching me. I can hear the compassion of those that care for me...while experiencing the blessing of hope that God allows them to give me. "This cup I drink from" is mine and if you know me...you know that I drink from it faithfully...

My dreams are still fulfilled and my life has great value. When the challenging times seek to overpower me...my sweeter blessings bring me comfort and renewed hope. It is then that my true faith is revealed...as my body regains strength from within. My family and friends know of "this cup I drink from" for each of them...have cups of their own...

March 14, 2010

"THIS TOO WILL PASS"

As a child, my grandparents, parents and family gave me many things that I needed for living. My parents gave me life...and that precious gift...my name. My family gave me a path to follow to be successful and advance my given family name. They gave me love, and cared for me, gave me protection, what I needed and so much more. However, I had a mind of my own and often thought that "this too will pass"...

Troubled I was as a child...and I sought not their way. For my reference point was pointed in a different way. I sit here in this place that they all wanted to keep me from being in. I carry most of the pain and understand the pain they also must be feeling. Yes, I brought shame to myself and tainted the family name...a shame that I can only blame on me...so I hope "this too will pass"...

I now have a choice I must make...and the price to be paid...only I will know. The loneliness and isolation will be hard on me, but the family will feel it too. My choice will be right this time...and God will get me through the situation I am in. I will use the hard lessons I am learning to align my reference with that of those that I love and that love me. For by the grace of God I know "this too will pass"...

"This too will pass" and I will put my bad behind the door marked history... then lock it with the key of understanding. I will swallow that key with a glass of hope...then walk away from it with a leap of faith. I will find the path of my father's footsteps...and walk in them knowing God will be with me...and never leave me alone. I will lie down to sleep each night covering myself...with that blanket of family love and sleep peacefully dreaming of a better tomorrow. I know I will wake each day by God opening the curtains of joy...so that my eyes can see the wonders He created. It is now that I am working on bettering me forevermore. Family, I am sorry for what I have done so please forgive me... pray for me and know "this too will pass"...

April 27, 2008

"TREES ON TIMOTHY LANE"

My last visit to 1153 Timothy Lane was a visit like most others. Alone, I walked the grounds of that piece of land I love. In the shadows cast by the home that's Mom and Dad's...I sat silently to reflect on life. Oh if the "trees on Timothy Lane" could talk...most of my thoughts would be revealed...

Many years ago a great man and woman used blood, sweat and tears of many years of work and oppression...to purchase this piece of land I love. They lived great lives and taught their children the true values to get them through life. Under the "trees on Timothy Lane" ...I too learned those values from them and those they had taught them to. Pop, I am so glad you taught us well...

Now that I am my grandfather's age when he died back in 1958...I know those values well. Lord, thank you for what they taught me...for now I can provide for others...and yes, I can teach those values too. When I come home the trip is not fulfilled until I spend some time...under the "trees on Timothy Lane". Just remembering when and reliving again...those family gatherings... and those lifelong precious memories that my family shares with me...

God let those "trees on Timothy Lane" mean to others the same thing that they mean to me...and when you close my eyes for the last time...a vision of those "trees on Timothy Lane" I want one last time to see...

November 28, 2008

"TRIED AND TESTED, BUT NEVER BESTED"

For many, life is lived with only minor setbacks and lots of joy. A life like that is good to live, but sometimes it lacks the excitement to make life an adventure. Not me, I was "tried and tested, but never bested"...

Growing up in a big family that was far below poverty status was no cup of tea. I thank God that it made me the person I have become today. I went from pigtails to perms, from pantaloons to silk nylons. All along the way, I was "tried and tested, but never bested"...

It took me longer than most, but my college degree I have now. It is only overshadowed by my CPA. Yes, you could say I have arrived. I'm eating high on the hog now, not feeding them. I have cars, jewels and fancy clothing too. I'm no longer envious of what others have. Many just don't understand how I have been "tried and tested, but never bested".

Hubby...and I have a business of our own, as well as a nice home. To those who ask, I thankfully say...be "tried and tested, but never bested". I am Sugar, big sister of the McDonald family and I love you all. My brothers and my sister...together, we have been "tried and tested, but never bested", let's stay that way for if we are divided we...can be bested...

April 28, 2009

"TWO RACQUETS, ONE FAMILY DREAM TO LIVE"

Although we were unknown to the world, it did not stop us from dreaming of reaching the status of being the best. Those "great ones" before us hardly knew our names and doubted the greatness of our game. They all would come to know us, for with each victory came more fame. We are "two racquets, one family dream to live"...

Our coach and father is not a traditional teacher and all others did not believe in how he taught us the game. With power, speed and a stronger will than most, we showed the world that color and being different didn't mean we could not win. Big sister Venus introduced us to the world and little sister Serena validated that we deserved to be recognized as the best. "Two racquets, one family dream to live" with each victorious swing we make...

Our victories over opponents are not just victories for us. They are victories for a family, faithful people and so much more. Be it together in doubles, solo against the world or even between just the two of us. Have no doubt that when Venus and Serena take the court it is "two racquets, one family dream to live, now and forevermore...

August 29, 2010

"WELCOME"

This is the house that we make our home...Comfort awaits you within these walls...Happiness lives here for love is shared by all...We always have room so we give freely...Joy is abundant, allowing us to live peacefully...Our hearts are right for we have faith in God...so with open arms we welcome you...to our home...

January 1, 2009

"WHEN I THINK OF YOU"

How I move forward to overcome adversity is my internal measure of my strength...and how I analyze each situation I face to find the right solution... is what makes me successful in life. "When I think of you"...a calmness comes over me and I have what I need to live...to move on...

Each day life's pressures increase just to challenge me. I know there is a need to improve how I deal with those pressures. It does not matter how many or what persons I surround myself with...for I must face my pressures all by my-self. "When I think of you"...I find the strength I need to convert those pressures into energy that keeps me strong...

How I relate to others is always there for others to see. There are no masks that can truly hide my soul...and the cover of night is more transparent than most think. "When I think of you"...I know how to love and care for others...I know how to give...and I know how to complete me. Mother, "When I think of you"...I know how I must live...and how much I have to give...

April 18, 2010

"WHY I REACH FOR THE SKY"

Yesterday was so amazing...that I had to remember all of the great things that happened to me. My thoughts are racing through my mind...but not as fast as my heart races to keep up with the excitement that my life brings me. No other person can feel what I do in the same way that I do...and that makes me unique...it also makes my life an endless adventure filled with excitement that I ache to live...to experience...

My great smile is a gift that I will always have and share with others as I live my life. My smile is so amazing that it draws others to me...it is then that I become more than me...for often I become hope for those needing comfort... and the benchmark for those wishing to achieve. Now I understand me and I know that tomorrow...I hope to still be amazing those that are around me with my smile and drive...to live a greater life...

When asked "why I reach for the sky"...I have only one response. First, my smile highlights my face and then I speak of how amazing my yesterdays were. It is then that my face transforms into a picture of confidence...framed by faith, hope and sincerity...

My secret...there is nothing more important to do each day than duplicate my efforts of yesterday...by reaching for those distant stars. Not those in the sky...but instead, those sparkling in the eyes of those looking back at me. You are "why I reach for the sky" and I pray that it will always be that way for me...

April 6, 2010

"YOUR BEST IS ENOUGH FOR ME"

A perfect dream has that perfect ending which leaves you wishing for more while it satisfies your every desire. Your presence has that same affect on others...so in my serenade to you I would say "your best is enough for me" don't change a thing...

Tall and slender as most women desire to be...with eyes so alluring that they deliver the purest message for others to see. Those softly spoken words can hypnotize others like those of the Greek Sirens...oh how they mesmerize me. "Your best is enough for me" for it makes me dream of an eternity with you... always there next to me...

Although beauty is not the most important thing to me, you have it and that is plain to see. Your lips are so inviting, that they must lead directly to your loving heart. They make me dream of them parting just enough to have our first kiss. Please oh please give me just one kiss that I can remember forevermore...a kiss that will make our passion soar...higher than the eagles we adore. In my heart I know "your best is enough for me" so that is why I treat you so respectfully. Oh, how I dream of the day that I hear your voice say..."your best is enough for me"...

December 18, 2010

SECTION III

LOVE AND FRIENDSHIP

"The symbols of love all can see...the feelings of love... only lovers know"...

"Friendship is a wonderful thing...its greatest highlight is falling in love"...

"A BRIDGE WE MUST BUILD"

I can only look at you through the broken window to my heart...there is too much pain to see you clearly with my eyes...or feel your love that is now just a distant memory...

I'm still drawn to those great memories of us, so in love, inseparable...lost without each other. So now here we are losers in the game of love. Living apart, looking for happiness...the same happiness that we stole from each other, not to be replaced, unparalleled...and never to be duplicated...

What happened to that love? Did the respect fade away, did life push us a part...or were we led by the temptation of having it all? Maybe nothing less would do. Was whatever it was, worth the pain...we now endure...

It may be foolish of me to think so simple...and I know you may want a better assurance than I have to offer. I'm offering me and all I have...is that not enough? Imperfect as I may be, I am willing to accept...your imperfectness as well...

Let the muddy waters flow under "a bridge that we must build" together. So while standing on that bridge...we can hold hands and fall in love all over again...

January 1, 2008

"A NEW STAR IN HEAVEN'S CHOIR"

Now, the stars bounce to the beat caused by your dancing feet. Yes, the children of Israel have picked up their harps to set under the weeping willows to join in the melody as Michael softly sings "The Man in The Mirror". In Heaven...the Angels are more joyful, for there is "a new star in Heaven's Choir"...

Michael kept singing his songs and entertaining to bring joy to us all. He collected the stones...that all threw at him on earth. Now those stones can be seen just below the surface of the Jordan River...and they are his stage now. I can visualize him moon walking on the water...singing "Remember the Time". Our greatest star is "a new star in Heaven's Choir"...

Life is "Dangerous" if you don't live right. It's "Human Nature" to "Wanna be Startin' Somethin'". The system is set...and it is hard to "Beat It". Trying to be a "Smooth Criminal" won't work...because you ain't "Bad". Tell me "Why you Wanna Trip on Me". Just listen to me "Jam"...and "Leave Me Alone" because I'm "a new star in Heaven's Choir"...

When St. Peter says "Give it to Me", I know I have to be a "Thriller". Momma always said ..."Keep the Faith" and sing to help "Heal the World". Life for me was like...living "In the Closet". Some said I didn't know if...I wanted to be "Black or White". Michael, most of us think you are "Gone Too Soon". All I know is that "The Way You Make Me Feel" means...there is "a new star in Heaven's Choir". Rest in peace Michael...knowing "I Just Can't Stop Loving You"...

July 12, 2009

"APPRECIATE ME FOR I WILL ALWAYS APPRECIATE THEE"

I cannot always control who I meet and the circumstances in which I meet them. I can only view the chance meeting as an opportunity that life has presented to me. I judge not the person for it is the actions of the person which determine their net worth to me. I ask not too much of others, just that you "appreciate me for I will always appreciate thee"...

My body may be beautiful but it may not always be so beautiful to thee. My hair may be beautiful for I can change it to please you and me. My heart is the true treasure that I can offer to thee. So "appreciate me for I will always appreciate thee" for that defines the true me...

My kindness is there to be shared. My joy is there to induce joy in others. My smile is there to soften whatever burdens you may be bearing. My touch brings affection as it absorbs the affection that others give. As I communicate, it is in hopes of bringing you memories you want to relive time and time again. Yes I am all about positivity and that is all that I ask you to give me. So "appreciate me for I will always appreciate thee" by sharing with you...the best I have to give...

August 14, 2010

"A VALENTINE GREETING"

On this day...may your heart be joyous as you share memories with those you love. May the memories of yesterday blend in with those of today...to lift your spirits and bring renewed hope of a joyous tomorrow...

Love and share love unconditionally...for only you know your heart and only you can allow others to share your joy...by bringing some joy to their lives...for material things only represent what others can receive from you. What you allow them to feel becomes a memory...the renewed hope of the joyous days to come...

Happy Valentine's Day...

February 7, 2010

"BEING HAPPY DOESN'T MEAN YOU'RE PERFECT"

In life there are many stories to be told. Those stories have to be lived first...to be meaningful and worth telling to someone. I always want to be able to tell the perfect story...a story with great purpose, wonderful dialog and the perfect ending. I am realistic so I know that "being happy doesn't mean you're perfect" so my stories seldom are...

I remember yesterday and use what I learnt to make me better today. I know of the trials and troubles that I have lived through...so I know what mistakes I have made along the way. Many no one else knows of and I plan to keep it that way. You see me displayed day after day in the scene that you wish for me. It is troubling sometime to act the parts...that others cast me in. "Being happy doesn't mean you're perfect" so I wish others would just...allow me to act out my own script...

"Being happy doesn't mean you're perfect"...it means that you've learnt to accept the imperfections. It means that inside I can achieve peace...while leaving the world to wonder how I do it. It means that tomorrow I will live for me...for my happiness is achieved by knowing myself. It means that the scripts others write for me...will never be acted out...I will be acting out my own. Mostly...it means that I know my perfection is something I must always live to achieve...

February 7, 2010

"DISTANCE"

Distance is no more than a glass wall...if that is what you see it as. When those you love are away from you...you need only to visualize their face...remember them fondly or relive some of the great memories you shared with them...to feel their presence...

So do not see distance as anything more than a glass wall. For when you get it right...that glass wall will appear the same as a mirror...and your reflection on the past will bring joy to you now...and forevermore...

June 15, 2008

"EARN ALL I HAVE BY GIVING ALL YOU GOT"

If I look into your eyes...I will see how you are looking at me...so your eyes must meet mine. They must show your strength and the passion inside you must be projected through them. If there is fear...it will be known by me. Deceit can't hide from these eyes of mine. In my eyes the message is clearly displayed...you must "earn all I have by giving all you got"...

In the softness of my voice...there is passion and so much strength. The pureness of my laughter is easy to hear...as it lets you know just how real I can be. I communicate with my voice as your voice speaks of you. If my voice is my weapon, my ears are my shield. They hear you and tell me so much more. I will always tell you to "earn all I have by giving all you got"...

If you "earn all I have by giving all you got" I will see it...and I will hear it too...and I will feel all that you communicate to me. For my heart to give... it must be satisfied with what it receives. You can know me...we can be great friends...but if you want my love, "earn all I have by giving all you got"...

August 30, 2009

"ETCH A MEMORY OF ME"

I am like I am for reasons that mean the world to me. I want you to remember me fondly, remember me truthfully. Remember me positively and remember me eternally. You see, I want you to "etch a memory of me" in your mind so you will remember me...

A smile is not costly. It is free to give and it causes fond memories, even if you don't know me. I give them with dignity for they are a great part of me. Please "etch a memory of me", cheerfully smiling at thee...

My eyes should not bring you misery. They should be fun for you to see. They are the entry of the tunnel to my heart. Caring, compassion and love you should see, when looking at me. Comfort and security should be there, when you "etch a memory of me" looking at thee...

In my arms is more than strength. They allow you to feel the true me. Be it a hand shake or a hug, it should be a memory you want to relive when you later think of me. "Etch a memory of me" and you will always be able to feel my presence when you remember me...

I know my character defines me, so I will be truthful, real, honest, loving and caring too. I know that throughout life others will remember me based on all that I do. If I touched you in some special way, you will always be able to picture me if you "etch a memory of me" in your heart...

December 20, 2009

"FEELING THE POWER OF LOVE"

On a normal day...life is much less complicated and just easier to live. Normal days are welcomed because those bad days exist. When those bad days are here we often find comfort in "feeling the power of love"...

When adversity comes not only to visit, but for a long stay in your life, you need comfort. When you find comfort, it is almost certain that you are usually "feeling the power of love"...

Are you "feeling the power of love" in your life and living to love so that others are "feeling the power of love" as well? When you feel love...are you able to give it back? Just relax and share "feeling the power of love"...

"Feeling the power of love" is a blessing from God. If you experience it you are not only blessed...you are also loved by someone. If you are providing that power, love...you are allowing another to experience "feeling the power of love"...

September 13, 2008

Stephen McDonald

"FEELINGS AND MEMORIES DO ENDURE"

Over the waves of the ocean, up the slopes of the mountains, through the valleys and thick forest growth they travel unseen or heard, but mostly unstoppable. They travel a path that only one's conscience knows. You see "feelings and memories do endure" for they are forever with you...

Through joy or pain they remain the same. Though masked by anger or a smile you force for others to see they are always with thee. Feelings and memories linger and stay in the home no one but you really ever enter for "feelings and memories do endure" secretly inside of you...

Let your heart love...while beauty, your eyes behold. Let your feelings show...or no one else will know. Bring joy to yourself so others know you will accept and share the joy they have too. Understood, desired or not... your memories will remind you of it all... then feelings come back to let you know that "feelings and memories do endure". No one else can tell because only you will truly know for sure...

May 29, 2010

"FOLLOW THE RAINBOW TO MY HEART"

Looking in the mirror...I see my reflection. People, I am just like you...till you look closer to see that I am unique...just like thee. Look through your clouds of confusion, through your flashes of hate and the droplets of despair...then ignore the roar of condemnation...visualize, then "follow the rainbow to my heart"...

The light and white colors you see...they are the softness in me. The yellow that you see...outlines the path to take...if you want to get to me. The grey and light blue that you see...lets you know I am approachable, and there are many ways to reach me. At this point I hope you can see...how to "follow the rainbow to my heart"...

Now the dark blue and the green you see...the dark blue is the depth of my soul...deep just like the sea and the green is how I grow those around me... and together they are the basic fiber of me. I must be anchored to be strong enough to lead...and to leave a path so you can "follow the rainbow to my heart"...

Now those bright colors, mostly the reds...they are there like beacons to attract you. Once they have your attention it is then you can see...red is for the passion in me. Passion comes from the heart which feeds all of me...so if you want to find that passion "follow the rainbow to my heart"...

December 13, 2008

"FREEZE THE MOMENT"

Looking westward the perfect sunset is there to be seen, to be shared with the one you love. "Freeze the moment" in your memory...so that you can enjoy it when the sunset is just a sunset...

After months of joy, and sometime pain, your child is born and you hear and see the child for the first time. "Freeze the moment" for there will...never be another moment like this one....

Life gives you so many chances to live...so if sorrow comes and is washed away by tears of joy...do not neglect to "freeze the moment" for that joy... brings your peaceful world back to you...

Missing your loved one is never easy...so thankfully memories are great comforters...and knowing that all is great between you is comforting too. So when your eyes lock on each other and you embrace, you will not be the only one wishing...if I could only "freeze the moment" my life would be perfect...not only now, but forevermore...

July 14, 2008

"GLADYS, THE ONLY SONGSTRESS FOR ME"

No one will understand how I feel even when so many probably feel the same way. I grew up listening to you and wanting to meet you one day. This is an old dream which I have relived so many nights as I slept...and it is odd, but each time I dream it... I find myself trying to get to where you are. In the end I find myself on the "midnight train to Georgia" for there...you can be found in the memories that I have of you...

You travel so many places that it is hard to know where you are. Long ago you traveled with your group in cars and buses and probably on trains too. As fame became attached to your name I am certain that planes are your chosen means for travel these days. Yesterday, "I heard it through the grapevine" that you were near...so I changed my plans in hopes of meeting you...and living a lifelong dream of mine...

Although "neither one of us" knows the other and I am sure knowing me is not something you have ever desired...a chance meeting is possible now. So here we are in the same place at the same time...I see, the stars have aligned for me. Maybe tomorrow you will remember me and smile if you do. I know that on each tomorrow my dreams of the past will be completed...for today I met you...the songstress I most admire. Your gift to me...be it just a smile, a glance or touching your hand...it now completes my dream and becomes a memory that I can relive...each day throughout eternity...

February 14, 2010

"HERE FOR YOU TO KNOW"

In my mind, I know I am a wonderful person...the mate that will make you happy...so you need only to prove you deserve me...

In my heart there is love, love unknown by me or others until I give and share it with you. In my body there is affection and the ability to...show that affection for you, so you need only to allow me to share all I am with you...

In my words there is great comfort because my word is my bond...and a reflection of all that I am. You need only to listen well...and you will learn of my heart...

In my smile there is warmth like that of a fire...yet it is better because...it comforts and never burns. You need only to allow that warmth to penetrate your heart...and heal the broken pieces. Then love will flow throughout your body...in search of mine...

In my touch there is more than contact...for the story of my life is being transferred to you. While I absorb the greatness in you...just touch me with the same purity to feel...the same greatness in me...

In my eyes you can see the past is behind me...and that I am ready to make my future the best days of my life. You need only to look into them to feel who I am...while allowing me to feel you in the same way. I am improving...because I need to make me better each day. I am "here for you to know"...so come share life with me...today, tomorrow and forevermore...

February 4, 2008

"HOW HARD IS IT TO LOVE ME"

When I have spare moments or just take a little time to think...I often wonder "how hard is it to love me". Am I worth the effort it takes...and is the benefit enough to endure what it takes...

If you look at me do you see the positive me...then when I speak do you want to stay or just run away? When I smile is it genuine or...can you see deceit in that smile. Looking in my eyes, now that is a true test...are they warm and trusting? Do they send a comforting message your way? "How hard is it to love me"...just as I am...

If I touch you...and the warmth is transferred to you. Does it make you feel rewarded? If I hold you in my arms, holding my body close to yours...does your body trust what it feels and welcome my touch...or maybe even ache for that touch to last? "How hard is it to love me"...when our bodies speak to each other...

At those moments when all is not well between us...you will truly know "how hard is it to love me", to forgive me...and to let me know that you still love me and will forevermore. "How hard is it to love me" this you should ask yourself and answer it truthfully. When you can truthfully answer "how hard is it to love me", you will know what it takes and what...you must give to be that better lover...that your lover's heart desires...

November 23, 2008

"HOW YOU LIVE LIFE IS AS IMPORTANT AS HOW YOU FEEL"

When you search for answers to why a relationship is not working out for you...and when the way you feel is not enough to comfort you...and when your lover feels the same way too...and when the two of you become more distant everyday and just don't seem to be able to get back to the happiness that you once enjoyed...it is time to realize that "how you live life is as important as how you feel" for love alone is never enough...

A great relationship requires several building blocks to be able to endure what life brings you. Often we leap over some of the important ones to get to the glamorous one...love. The foundation of love is built of some of these blocks. Comparability is the glue...trust, compromising, friendship and the desire to be together, all form the foundation...so "how you live life is as important as how you feel"...

Respect, compassion, faith and hope cover and protect love from what life brings your way. Now life...how you live it is the key...Those that don't dream... find it hard to have goals. Those that are not faithful...never learn to truly trust. Those that are selfish...are not capable of compromising or showing compassion. Any of these character flaws weaken love's foundation and protective covering...so next time you get the chance...get to know the person, because "how you live life is as important as how you feel" about each other...

December 27, 2010

"I AM TROUBLED"

I'm at an age where I know how to think...and how to find the answers I need. I know me, my body, my faith and also my needs. So why does my Heart...keep fighting with the logical me...

I know what is right, but what I want is not always what is right. Just give me peace of mind and comfort my heart...for lives are for sharing and not tearing apart...

If it was me, how would I feel...how would I deal with another suitor after my lover's heart? I am troubled for I must think of me and do what must be done...to please me...

August 28, 2007

"I NEVER HAVE TO"

I watch others as they struggle to cope with their lives and it reminds me of how I once struggled too...struggled to find myself and the best in others as well. Love came before in my life only to be shattered as our struggles made us grow apart. Now "I never have to" struggle anymore for you are the love of my life...

Your thoughtfulness is often over looked for we always look for more excitement in our lives. I see how you teach our children. Only a dedicated father and caregiver can do it so well and accept so little in return. You are a real man that the community knows they can depend on, just as we; your family does each day. You see "I never have to" be concerned about tomorrow because you allow me to plan it with you each and every day...

You are my protector in so many ways that words don't come close to expressing my feelings about you. Only my actions come close to letting you know how I truly feel. Time is precious to us all, yet I give that to you continually. Love is not manufactured, it is birthed from genuine feeling...the desire to care and the joy I feel in having you in my life. I know "I never have to" worry about where you are or what you are doing for your dedication is to me and your family. I love you and I always will...

March 30, 2011

"I WILL ALWAYS REMEMBER LOVING YOU"

It may have started as a chance meeting; thankfully...it turned out to be a great loving relationship. When our eyes meet it is easy to see...there is a special true love. When we choose to touch, there is always a moment of awkwardness... for we must become one...to truly enjoy the moment...

As our bodies anticipate becoming one...they move to each other for that first kiss...that moment we long for always. Yes, together again one body with two souls. In your arms there is warmth...even in the coldest times of our lives. Just the right pressure in the right places...allows our bodies to become one. We are in our own world now...while living in the world with the rest...

Memories are the greatest treasures of our lives...so we live new memories with each minute we are together. We are just normal people, not famous and not well known...but we know each other and...that is all the fame we need. Other treasures we have and sometimes, we lose them...yet the memories we share we never worry about losing...for they are our shared treasures... treasures forevermore...

Time will age us and yes, it is possible that...one day we will part. You are forever a part of me and you are...forever in my heart. I will love you forever... because "I will always remember loving you"...

April 11, 2009

"I WILL LOVE TOMORROW"

"I will love tomorrow" because you will be there with me...I'm lying here next to you...having no fear of going to sleep...for I know I will dream of you as the highlight of my memories of today. I am thinking only of you, so calmly I will sleep through the night...yes, I can feel you next to me... which gives me the promise of...waking next to you when tomorrow comes...

I wake in the middle of the night...just to watch you...for I did not spend enough time with you yesterday. When I am satisfied within...I can sleep again...but I'm dreaming of holding you in my arms...when the morning comes. "I will love tomorrow", so I can learn...to love you even more...

It saddens me when we have to part for our daily journeys. Sadly, I take my memories of us together...and walk away. I know that later when I see you... we'll just fall deeper in love...to love each other more. Our hearts beat as one when we are together and...I know "I will love tomorrow" for tomorrow...you will be the love of my life...

"I will love tomorrow" when in Heaven...we meet to fall deeper in love. There, we will love each other the way it was meant to be. I can see the angels gathering around us...just to see how true love should be. "I will love tomorrow" because...I will be loving you for eternity...

December 6, 2008

"IF I COULD"

"If I could" be like a cloud in the sky, I would shower you with love, fill your life with goodness and protect you from the dangers that trouble your mind...

"If I could" hold you in my arms, I would warm your body with the love of my heart, shield you from your fears within so that we can share our strengths each and every day...

"If I could" see your smile, I know your kindness would be revealed. I would be enriched by your greatness and your faith would provide the hope I need to journey on...

"If I could" kiss your lips, I know the memories of our yesterdays would flood my thoughts, bring me renewed hope of living today with you while allowing me to dream of loving you each tomorrow to come...

"If I could" capture that moment in time, I would be happier with each breath that I take. "If I could", I would, show you the ways I would keep loving you forevermore...

October 16, 2011

"IF I NEVER KNOW HOW MUCH I CAN LOVE YOU"

When we kissed that first time, there was fear and oh...so much to learn about each other. We knew each other, but now we had to explore each other...trying to find the depth of our souls. It was all so exciting for each day...we were rewarded with sharing more love and great memories. I thought to myself "if I never know how much I can love you" we can have new special memories forevermore...

Once we knew we were in love with each other...we knew no others could change how we loved each other. We knew to depend on each other...for we could not live without the love of the other. The world presented us with daily mysteries and so many challenges to conquer. We became so programmed to know when and to look forward to the end of events, trials and troubles. But I was always comforted by asking myself "if I never know how much I can love you" then I have no ending or goals to achieve except loving you more and more each day...

"If I never know how much I can love you" I can never stop trying to love you more. I can always look to tomorrow and the adventures we can share. I can give you all of me faithfully...for I know God will give me more in return. I know happiness and joy will comfort me forever..."if I never know how much I can love you". And I know if I asked...you would say "if I never know how much I can love you" I would always look forward to what tomorrow brings us...

March 13, 2011

"IF I PAINTED YOUR PICTURE"

When I am near you my imagination runs wild for you provoke thoughts such as the story about Helen of Troy. It is recorded that she launched a 1000 ships and started a war. That pales in comparison to my experience with you thus far. "If I painted your picture" there would be passion for the thousands of hearts that you have touched in your special way. That is the type of power that no one can conquer, so I just admire...

Your eyes tell of your loving soul as they sparkle like the stars at night. They are sultry and they seduce with their every glance, stirring the passion of my souls. "If I painted your picture" I would use silky red strokes to express how you captured my greatest resource, my beating heart...

Any room is your stage and all eyes follow your every move like devoted fans, for they seek that chance adventure of sharing living memories with you for many tomorrows to come. "If I painted your picture" the sun would be shining, giving me hope of sharing that perfect sunset in your arms...

Your beauty is natural so nature's greatest creations just highlight it so well. There is strength in your every action promising that you can endure the journey through life and give pleasure, love and so much more. "If I painted your picture" it would truly never be completed, for you will always inspire more strokes to paint the picture of the amazing person you are destined to become...

November 5, 2011

"IF WE FALL IN LOVE"

A trip down memory lane is traveled in one's memory and all memories are relived again...the good and the bad all make those special memories worth reliving again...

"If we fall in love" can we share a last name...can we live together with little to no change...can our hearts beat as one and...can we both remain sane?...

"If we fall in love" are you willing to do more...more than love me? Are you willing to want me as well,...are you willing to compromise too and...say you are mine...

"If we fall in love" our worlds will have to become one...so we must trust each other in times of trouble. I will need you...need you to hold my hand...need you to walk our path...and need you to bring me joy and comfort too. I will need you to always be there...with me no matter what...

"If we fall in love" the journey will have just begun...so love will not be enough to see us thru...for others and the world will test our love. Without trust, respect, peace of mind and...a great friendship too...being in love will not be enough. Our plan for life has to be much, much more than love alone. So "if we fall in love" please understand...that sharing a name requires so much more...

October 5, 2008

"I'M ENJOYING YOU"

Expectations are not the same for me as they are for you...for my need to be satisfied must be provided and I wish the same for you too...

The manual on how to love, no one has written. The manuals to help you through relationships... do exist. Read them once or a thousand times and you will get better at relating...but true love will still be hard to find...

Emotions make relating a difficult task...for you can only control yours some-times and...never control those of another. Feelings, oh feelings how are thou defined....where do you really come from? From the heart most will say...and that seems to be the answer till the relationship is challenged by...that emo-tional rainstorm one day. You then will pray...sunshine, oh sunshine of hope come light up my life...

Time is the helping hand that we often refuse to reach out to...when we are confused or stuck in the muck of uncertainty. Just remember that time allows you to learn of others...that which you do not know...

Talking and listening is how secrets are revealed...early in a relationship when there are so many unknowns...unknowns which can and will...make the dif-ference one day. Stop declaring you are in love and...learn to say "I'm enjoying you" and just hope that the other person is enjoying you too...

Time, yes it will pass...questions, yes they will be asked...listening, yes it will be done...and then at some special moment in the sunshine of hope...love will come faithfully...yes even at a time you see as your darkest hour...

Be like the farmer that has planted a seed. Watch it...care for it and let it grow. Soon the fruit of your emotional labor will grow in your heart...and blossom into passionate love. Now you can say...I love you and it will be easier to say "I'm enjoying you"...

August 3, 2008

"IN A MOMENT"
(A bride's thoughts on the wedding day)

In a moment...we became one. One love and one family...with one common mission to have...one life to live...

In a moment...the old book of my life was finished...closed forevermore...for now I write my best book of my life...no, our life...

In a moment...all my dreams, my goals, my needs were satisfied with you and

I becoming one...one family, one book of life and...one life to live...

In a moment...that hopefully you all have known...or someday will know just how we felt...that moment we knew our love was forevermore...

In a moment...that will last a life time...there will be endless moments, like this moment that all make this moment...an eternity living as one...

June 16, 2007

"IN TIME"

In time, the distance between our souls will become only a thin line of reality...

In time, the memory of our yesterday will pale in comparison to our dreams for tomorrow...

In time, that first kiss will be behind us...as we share so many more...

It is then that, time will stand still...as our forever together is lived, forevermore...

May 22, 2007

"IT'S FLOWING NOW"

I am so much better now...for once back then...the drought had the best of me and I had to use most of the joy I had...just keeping myself happy day after day...

The light in my eyes had lost most of its sparkle...from trying to hide the tracks of my tears. Due to my thoughts wandering around on an unknown path...my faith in love was lost in the jungle of sadness...

Oh, how I worked to keep my body ready for that perfect touch, caress...and loving moment. I used all my strength to keep me wanting...that perfect loving feeling...

That ole sun, it kept on shining...trying to dry out my soul. The miracle I prayed for...it appears to be here now...for someone has brought that nourishing love back to my life. Yes, "it's flowing now"...

"It's flowing now" so my eyes have that sparkle again...my joy is plentiful and...that jungle of sadness is washing away. I got that loving feeling I want...and my heart is working just right again. Happily I say, "it's flowing now" for my heart is loving again...

July 5, 2008

"JUST ALLOW ME TO SING YOU MY LOVE SONG"

When your day is not all that you dreamed of last night...and something keeps getting in your way when you try to bring back that joy you love to feel, the joy that comforts you. And when the lights keep reminding you of how the sunshine brightens up your day and warms your body even on the coldest night... then "just allow me to sing you my love song" so that your memory of me never fades away...

   Just when the world seems to be closing in on you and your thoughts are so troubled that they make you long for a better life. When that reflection in the mirror doesn't comfort you...for you know inside, that the image you see is just a shadow of who you really want to be...Don't lose faith and don't wait for others to make it better...I hope that you will remember to .."just allow me to sing you my love song" of how we will love each other forevermore...

   "Just allow me to sing you my love song" of how many ways I will love you. Let my song tell you of the tomorrows that we will love each other even more. Listen to the softness of my voice as the love reaches out to you...and feel the rhythm that is driven by the emotions within me. Oh, "just allow me to sing you my love song" it is my special...my perfect love offering to you...

December 23, 2010

"LOVE"

For the right reasons...in just the right moment in time...
   Life takes a right move and all is right...
   The heart is beating to a drum that only a lover understands...
   Love...it makes the heart beat just right so the soul knows...that what you are feeling is all real!

May 22, 2007

"LOVE IS A VAST EMOTION"

When you stand at the foot of the mountains, your journey to the top can be visualized, but only realized if you are standing on top of the mountain. As you stand on the ocean's shore looking at the horizon where the sky appears to touch the distant waters, you cannot see the distant shore for you can only see it if you cross the water and stand on that shore...

In life, we have many wants and desires and seldom are they more important to us than love. Like the mountains and the ocean, love is challenging. For "love is a vast emotion" just wanting it will never allow you to experience its true feeling...

It starts as a chance encounter, grows to a desire to be friends. Then leaps the invisible barrier to become infatuation and finally works its magic on your mind and heart. Wow, it is now love...you are standing at the foot of the mountain or at the ocean's shore. Just remember "love is a vast emotion" and the journey to eternity together is not just a thought or a dream that comes true. It is an emotional journey you must plan together to climb the slippery cliffs and sail the treacherous waters...

That may sound easy, but that is not the case. For the journey is unknown and you know not what it takes for "love is a vast emotion" that grows inside you for someone that wants to make the journey with you. Forget not the fears and other emotions you must overcome and never underestimate the outsiders' desires to complicate your journey. "Love is a vast emotion" that is a fragile path to happiness in life shared on a journey to eternity together...

"Love is a vast emotion", so always know your journey is the one to make and that you can trust your partner. Know when the path is a dead end, when loving friendship is enough. Mostly, know there is no shame if you cannot make the chosen journey, because other opportunities will come. "Love is a vast emotion", climbers read the rocks and sailors study the skies so your journey to emotional bliss ends with you standing together on the mountain top looking at the distant ocean shore, knowing you are in love...

October 19, 2008

"LOVE, NOT JUST A WORD"

Love is not just a word; love is many things that most people do not understand. It is easy to understand and need love...but it is much harder to love...

Why...because it requires more than most know they are willing to give! So when you love...know that it is more than a feeling...it is everything and should last forevermore...

November 20, 2007

"LOVING FEELING LIBERATES THE HEART"

Lying here with my face buried in my pillow the tears I am shedding, not even I want to see. They roll down my cheeks and I know the pain that caused them could be with me for a long time. I now know what life is about and I wish I knew back then that a "loving feeling liberates the heart"...

Pain is just the emotion caused by my reaction to that which matters. I want to control feeling pain and how long it last but I can't. I should know me and how to mend what hurts me. So what challenges me is why it is that I have allowed it to be as it is. Now I know, a "loving feeling liberates the heart" to allow me to love unconditionally...

Yes that ole fear he kept me from living as I wanted. I feared the ending so I refused to give love a chance, ironically the hurt and pain I feared could come, I am experiencing. I have learned that a "loving feeling liberates the heart" and keeps my fears away...

Hurt and pain, yes I brought to myself because I knew not what tomorrow could bring. That is why I never gave being in love a try. Maybe being in love would have made tomorrow less fearful, less painful. Now that I know that a "loving feeling liberates the heart", I am certain that when faced with the decision again, I will fall in love forevermore...

May 31, 2008

"MEET ME AT THE RIGHT TIME AND PLACE"

I can see the passion in your eyes, feel the rhythm in your body and I sense the desire in your touch. I feel it in me and can tell that you can feel mine too. No words need to be spoken to tell each other what to do for the communication is clearly stated by our bodies. To each other they say "meet me at the right time and place"...

Our bodies, silently they communicate in a language not heard, it is only felt. It is a language not written in verse, yet every passage rhymes in harmony with the rest. A language reserved for lover and simple sex can never speak it this clearly. "Meet me at the right time and place", I want to feel your lips on mine, feel you holding me closely while touching the right spot at just the right time and oh, just right. Yes I hear yours clearly and I can tell it is listening to mine ...

That sensual touch oh yes that's it. Now couple your body to mine. I can feel how excitingly your body's rhythm matches mind. Our bodies are speaking silently and yes I can feel that we truly understand each other well. Please, don't ever stop for my body is still screaming "meet me at the right time and place"...

June 21, 2008

"MY FAVORITE VIEW INCLUDES YOU"

Life is lived and we all do it basically the same way so don't complicate it man. Look at your hands or your reflection in the mirror and you will see what life is, you will see you and hopefully see an acceptable you...

Seeing you is not enough, you must see all there is and then you will see the true you. Standing at the rail looking over the house tops I see the distant houses and all that God created and how man changed it. Oh, now I can see more, I see the distant islands and the great Atlantic. They remind me that life will test me and surviving depends on my life skills...

You see the beauty that nature uses to balance the world we know. Yes, I see more than that beauty. I see the reflection of your soul. Obedient to God, admired by many and trusted by those that love and respect you. You are ready and willing to give that you have and to help those needing a helping hand...

The wind bends the trees as the ocean erodes the shores and the sun bakes the land. This all happens as man stands helpless to change any of it. Yet it is all necessary for that is what created most of my favorite view. You see, "my favorite view includes you", standing in the foreground filling the picture with a loving smile, a joyous laugh, a look of comfort and the promise of an affectionate kiss waiting for me...

In nature's beauty we find ourselves for nature's beauty demands our best. Being alone, yes you can take it in by enjoying the soft music she plays. Just smell the freshness she brings each day and see how magnificent she is to just realize how small you really are...

Mostly, you should experience the comfort she gives and if you feel blessed to know me like I feel to know you, then you will always understand that "my favorite view includes you"...

October 26, 2008

"MY LOVE IS MY GREATEST TREASURE"

Why life is wonderful for me is no great secret. How my family has always cared for me is a treasure that last a lifetime. My life has always presented me with choices which have always defined my character, when I chose to live it my way. I have always been blessed to know that "my love is my greatest treasure" so I love unconditionally...

Love is not always joyous and some love that I shared, those closest to me did not understand or approve. Some love led me to adventures while others brought me tears and grief. When I go back down memory lane, I smile and I cry as each memory is relived. Yet, I still believe "my love is my greatest treasure" for it has always comforted me...

My love is a treasure that no one can steal. No matter how much I give, I always have more love to give. No matter how much I receive, I always have more room in my heart to accept the love others give me. I can feel the emotions, I can see the beauty and I experience its greatness each day. "My love is my greatest treasure" for it keeps me seeking love...day after day...

October 23, 2010

"MY TRUE LOVE SONG"

If you can understand "my true love song"...you are very special to me, for "my true love song" has a secret melody. You can only hear it if you are listening to my heart beating like a drum. Can you hear how the drums change their rhythm with just the promise of your touch? Can you hear the tenors raise their voices joyously as you take me in your arms? Listen closely my love... listen to "my true love song"...

Too many instruments will distort the melody so no horns, strings or keys are in my orchestra. Other voices will destroy the pureness of my melody so there is no choir. Since no others would understand the meaning of my melody...I sing "my true love song" so only you can hear. I know that you can hear it...if you are near or far...for I even hear your melody in my dreams...

I think our two melodies have become one...for I can hear just one melody when I am in your arms. Sometimes I hear a faint melody of someone else's drum...but their rhythm doesn't match mine as your true love song does...as it blends with my heart in singing "my true love song"...a melody that only two hearts in love with each other can understand to sing...

December 26, 2010

"MY VISION OF TOMORROW"

To some, today is considered my most special day for I am getting married. I truly know how important it is for one of God's Angels blessed me to have "my vision of tomorrow" on yesterday. I saw me walking from the shadows of yesterday's disappointments into the brightness of our dreams of loving each other on each tomorrow to come…

Can you see the passion in my eyes…can you hear my heart beating in anticipation…does the glow of my cheeks warm your heart…and does the sight of me make your soul reach out to the one you love. This was my vision of today that leads me to "my vision of tomorrow", our journey to eternity…

If living had not been so challenging on yesterday, I would not be prepared to journey on our adventures of tomorrow. For it will take the strength of both of us, to protect the love in our home. We will need our families and the grace of God to live our lives as one. See "my vision of tomorrow" has me loving you forever…filling each day with memories that we will treasure forevermore…

March 15, 2011

"NEW DREAMS I SEE"

If one could only see them up close they would understand as I do. The ocean is vast, but not as vast as what I see. The ocean is also deep for sure, so deep that it's depth in not truly known. I see a similar depth in thee, for "new dreams I see" in your eyes…

A chance meeting rewarded me. Casual conversation delivered me. A simple jester of kindness led me to this treasure. This treasure one finds only if you let them see. Yes up close they reveal that, within you there is so much more. Truly it is "new dreams I see" as your eyes look at me…

Most think they are just used to see. Not I, for there is a greater depth in me. There must be a light source like the sun that shines behind them, for they sparkle when they focus on me. There are "New dreams I see" because of the way you are smiling at me…

Their color is unique for all to see, a color like your homeland that is surrounded by the sea. They are exciting like your birth must have been as your mom delivered thee. There are "New dreams I see" dreams I hope I will get to know you well enough to see…

July 4, 2009

"NOT JUST KIND WORDS"

I touched your heart with words that I did not read some place or copy. The phrases, they are mine and they came from my heart...

Just think of what life would be like if there were no kind words. Would our hearts understand to love or care...would our hearts be able to feel the love that is given to us...

I am not interested in knowing how life would be without speaking or hearing kind words, without giving or feeling true love...Are you...

December 30, 2009

"OH MIGHTY KNIGHT"

I try to sleep, but I just toss and turn for you are weighing heavy on my mind. Yes you captured my heart so many years ago and I love you so. "Oh mighty Knight" take my heart with you into battle and allow it to shield you from danger by giving you a greater reason to return to me...

On my knees, I ask God to bless thee. I ask not for riches that you may bring me. I ask not for a great honor for thee. I ask not for a victory, but only for peace for you and me. "Oh mighty knight" I just want you to love and protect me as I love and take care of thee...

I cannot enjoy what you have given me, for my tears and empty arms are haunting me. I cannot sleep either, for the place that you sleep is cold for you are not there. The children ask questions, that I cannot always answer truthfully. Oh how I hope they cannot see, the fear in my eyes. "Oh mighty knight" as you fight for us, I hope you know that we love you...

"Oh mighty knight" upon your return, I will be able to breeze again. I can again share great moments when you are back with us. I can again sleep in your loving arms. And I can give you the love that is in my heart...my heart that you take with thee into battle as you fight to protect me. My heart that you then return to me...so that I can love you forevermore...

September 3, 2011

"ONLY REAL LOVE SURVIVES THE EMOTIONAL STORMS"

When you think that love is real you want it to last. Not just today and to-morrow, but for all of the tomorrows to come. You have two hearts, two minds and two sets of emotions which must always be in concert with each other for love to grow and bring you joy each day. Always be aware that "only real love survives the emotional storms" that each heart must endure...

Love is a feeling which has no true means of being measured. It is exposed to all that the world and others are capable of doing. You cannot control many things...no not even your own emotions. Circumstances and situations have a great influence on how you feel which influences your emotions. There is instability everywhere so "only real love survives the emotional storms" that happen each and every day...

Excitement is a constant that only needs a little coldness, like deceit...mixed with some heat, like anger...to become an unstable environment. When you mix a little lifting energy, like that generated by a broken promise...you have an emotional storm brewing. It brews more and more for hurt keeps lifting it until all hell breaks out...letting you know that this is a fierce emotional storm. Not much can stop the storm's fierceness so it is now...that you will know how strong your love truly is. "Only real love survives the emotional storms" so hope your love sees the rainbow as each storm passes on...giving way to another sunny day...

October 30, 2010

"ORGASM"

Is it just a dream or does it really feel this good. Am I able to understand what continues to happen to me? Will I remember this feeling always, or should I take it all in right now. Time seemed to stand still. I wanted to move yet nothing would allow it to happen. Am I passing out, oh I am so close that it frighten me. But the fear of this feeling disappearing is much more frighten-ing to me...

Just hold me I heard my voice say, in a voice that I know is mine yet it sounds too satisfied to really be coming from me. Wow, yes there are tears running down my cheeks. What is happening to me to make me feel this way? Sex is not new to me and I have felt similarly before, but this feeling is overwhelming, blinding and exhausting, yet I long for more...

I want to open my eyes to see if it helps me to understand. No, I am too afraid that it may change the great way that I feel. Wait, yes I hear my lover and know the experience is being shared. It comforts me to know this and momentarily I lose track of my own feeling of a blissful, unparalleled emotional high...

Wait a minute, I think I am beginning to come back to my normal self. As I do, things become much clearer. I now understand that I just experienced the greatest climax of my life. An "orgasm", no not just one but several chained together just masked as one. Now I am ready for many more of the same for an "orgasm" like that keep you wanting for more, more orgasms, more bliss and more perfect loving moments...

June 26, 2008

"RESERVATIONS FOREVER IN MY HEART"

There is no need to check or ask for a confirmation. There is no reason you should grow concerned or wait. There is no way someone else would be chosen over you. Your love has "reservations forever in my heart"...

There are no hours, minutes or seconds when your love cannot get to my heart. There are no circumstances when your love would be pushed away. There are no other hearts or loves that could ever mean more to my heart than your love. That is why your love has "reservations forever in my heart"...

I guarded my heart with all that my thoughts could control. This still did not protect it from those times when it was broken by pretenders. It is strong so it always recovered from the misery of being broken. I knew there was that perfect love that had "reservations forever in my heart"...

That allowed my heart to receive a love like yours, the only love for me to share. Your love has "reservations forever in my heart" and I know if others ask you would say. My heart has reservations for only one love, the only love that has "reservations forever in my heart" ...

January 1, 2010

"ROMANTICISM"

I slept peacefully last night for the last vision I had before closing my eyes was of you. I dreamed of lasting feelings, yes love was overflowing within causing my heart to care and giving me the desire to be with you always. "Romanticism" gives me a life, a reason to welcome tomorrow and the tomorrows to come...

I hope that tomorrow will be all I need and all I dreamed. I work to find love to have forevermore. For me "romanticism" is not just a good time here and now, it is everything for it leads to love forevermore. It is the only thing which will please me and bring peace to my heart...

The heart would not long for "romanticism" if it was not good for the soul. It would not be excited so in anticipation of the joy that love brings. It would not feel troubled when losing love that it has grown to share. Oh how refreshing "romanticism" is...to a once broken heart...

"Romanticism" is not meant to cost you anything. It is to give you that which you cannot have when you are alone. You get to dream of love and so much more. You get to live a life where tomorrow always brings you joy. Mostly, when love is shared, your "romanticism" flourishes so that all are aware...

May 29, 2010

"SENSUAL"

Only a chance meeting can affect me so. I imagine the mystery then watch it unfold. What sparks a romance is different for us all. Sometimes, you just have to allow it to happen, that all...

I open my lips to speak and that opens my heart. My eyes receive your messages as my heart sends out messages too. Hopefully, they are "sensual" to you...

My body is always ready as it promises you all I have to give. My lips always create that promise of a smile, a silent signal, inviting you, daring you to come closer to explore...

Words, yes I speak them too, just to break the silence in hope that you want hear my beating heart. "Sensual", yes I am, it allows me to charm you, while promising so much more...

October 29, 2011

"THE RIGHT LOVER SATISFIES THE HEART AND SOUL"

Only "the right lover satisfies the heart and soul" all others only come close. They get most of it right, leaving the rest to be desired. The right lover gives you all you ever wanted...

It's another sleepless night resulting from a little fight so you think, why should loving another be like this? If your lover doesn't talk till it is alright, that lover is just not right. Seek till you find the right lover for you, because "the right lover satisfies the heart and soul"...

Wondering where your lover has been while you sit waiting and wishing all is well. If it was this way on yesterday, what will have changed today? Will your face give your suspicions away and will you have the nerve to say, lover where have you been or lover do you want this to end? Deep within your heart you already know that only "the right lover satisfies the heart and soul"...

With the right lover you still cry, but they are tears of joy. Sometimes you still wait, but with anticipation of that first touch. Often you still ache, but with the desire that only your lover satisfies. "The right lover satisfies the heart and soul" and that is why the wrong lover doesn't and never will...satisfy your heart and soul...

December 13, 2008

"THE STORM IS ALWAYS JUST A MOMENT AWAY"

It is so wonderful to be in love and to have that special one in your life. It is so calming to see that your special one sees you as that special one too. With happiness comes comfort and with comfort comes the tendency to be less focused on that which you should be interested in...the true love of your life...

True relationships have so much more than love...for there is a greater need than love. Unfortunately, so many never truly consider this greater need and that is why "the storm is always just a moment away"...

You need a greater understanding and knowledge of each other. There must be common goals and objectives. Now beliefs are all very important as well. You need them all because "the storm is always just a moment away" and...you must always shelter your love...

The storm invades your loving because you leave too many ways for it to get in. You lack trust...so you keep pushing for changes that you yourself will not consider doing. You want that perfect mate...while doing little to become that special mate as well. This creates a very cloudy and unstable environment so "the storm is always just a moment away" and...that first lightning strike lets you know it's too late ...

As you wait for the lightning to strike you feel fear. You are anxious about protecting yourself...for you know the storm is upon you. Confused and disappointed you realize that...at these times love becomes just a feeling...for the lover that feels that greater need to...just protect their heart and honor...

August 30, 2008

"TODAY WE MARRY, TOMORROW WE ARE ONE"

I think of back to when we were just two persons...looking for that right person with whom to share the rest of our lives. Those endless days of hoping... which were shattered by broken promises and deceit of those we trusted. Finally, we have put that all behind us, so "today we marry, tomorrow we are one"...

I have gathered all of the pieces of my broken heart and you have helped me put them back together...as I helped you put yours back together as well. So now that we are in love, we know how to care, protect and...mend our broken hearts...and we now know how to care for them too...for we are one heart now. We know this is the right thing to do...so take my hand "today we marry, tomorrow we are one"...

For the first time we will wake tomorrow with the same name...just to live together with no shame. We will make a house a home...to build a family that will never bring shame to our name. We will never leave each other alone...so come share life with me, "today we marry, tomorrow we are one"...

As the sun sets each day, we will watch it together...and as tomorrow becomes today...we will plan tomorrow all over again. Pain will come and the joy of having you...will overshadow it. Love will remain abundant for...our hearts are now one. Despair will visit our lives and we will faithfully move around it, for love, trust and peace of mind...will always shield our love. It is time for all to know and witness...so "today we marry, tomorrow we are one"...

May 10, 2009

"TRUE POWER"

When we think of power, we almost always think of strength or wealth. It is admired by most and so many hope to be considered powerful one day. Someone wrote "the pen is mightier than the sword" for they understood what "true power" really is. Another took it further to say "a picture is worth a 1000 words". Both sayings are as truthful, as they are famous, for a picture is "true power" displayed for all to see...

The mind is a great collector of "true power" for it records all that it sees and it creates pictures for others to see. More importantly, it can record unspoken words, pictures of emotions and affection, pictures we cannot always put into words, "true power" generated by the heart...

We are defenseless when facing messages seen in others eyes. Try putting into words how you feel and all that you think of, when you are greeted with a smile. Try embracing in a hug and you will see how the words flood your mind, pictures that even 10,000 words cannot describe. So when you think of strength or wealth, realize that both are great to have. Just realize that they cannot match the "true power" of eyes, smiles, hugs and kisses, for they are the power that generates the feeling of love...

October 29, 2011

"TRUST ME TO LOVE YOU BACK"

On the surface the grass all looks the same and all the blades seek the rays of the sun...and bend to be closer to it. While beneath the beauty we see, each blade is attached to a stem...that is fed the nutrients Mother Earth provides... by the roots that never cease to grow. Those roots, if they could talk, would say, "trust me to love you back" my blades...

In relationships what we see or feel on the surface is not always...all that matters. Kindness is a great mask for love...whereas, respect, honesty and dependability are often overshadowed...by one's fear. Another's emotions can be faked over and over again...so I ask you to..."trust me to love you back" my love...for in me resides lasting love...

The two of us must make it work together as if we are one. I fear tomorrow just as you and I feel pain and...unwanted at times too. I focus on that which matters...love, respect, kindness, compassion, faith and hope...so that is why I can say "trust me to love you back" and...don't let our love slip away...

June 15, 2008

"YOU ARE THERE IN MY DREAMS"

As I open my eyes in hope of seeing you, I must give up dreaming of you. How blessed I am to live my dreams each day that I am with you. There are no tears for what I lose each time I wake, for the physical you is so much better for me. "You are there in my dreams" keeping me happy until I see you again...

Time is measured, yet it is endless and it is constant. There are no slow days or fast moments; those are only in our minds. As we rush we waste so many special moments which could be endless memories. "You are there in my dreams" just as constant as time, yet much more rewarding for each time I wake you are with me, making my dreams come true...

When I think of tomorrow, I smile for you are with me always. I am at peace for I know your love will comfort me. I am excited for I know I can keep living to love you. "You are there in my dreams" tomorrow and for the endless tomorrows to come. There to love me, be with me and complete me. "You are there in my dreams" for I know you dream only of loving me...

November 19, 2011

"YOU MAY BUILD IT, BUT IT TAKES LOVE TO BE"

In the darkness all that you have, dream of and work to achieve is just what you are building for yourself. "You may build it, but it takes love to be" happy in life. Love is the bonding agent that God has provided to keep us together...

If you are lost in your thoughts about what you have achieved, you may find comfort in knowing that others are wishing to be so blessed. You may even help some of them by sharing your wealth or wisdom. "You may build it, but it takes love to be" a comforter to those in need or be an inspiration to those that have lost their way...

Just look at all that you have and are known to have accomplished. Where is your balance, your mate to share it all and tell you that "you may build it, but it takes love to be" all that I desire and the mate that makes my life joyous? Love is desired by all so work to build a loving relationship as you work to build all that you dream of or desire to achieve...

July 4, 2011

82

VALENTINE'S DAY 2010

Let beauty always be defined by what I see when I am looking into your eyes, then even deeper into your soul. Let comfort always be what I feel when I am holding you while the excitement builds from within my soul. Let love be my best gift that I give you and the greatest gift that I ever receive from you...

My heart is joyous this day for I have in you all that a relationship with a lover can provide me. With great excitement...I dream of tomorrow when I renew my dedication to loving you. A love that time and troubles will test...and I will prove it is true...true love for only you...

Happy Valentine's Day...

January 31, 2010

VALENTINE'S DAY 2011

On special days we want special memories ...those special memories that we can cherish...

Allow your heart to give as much as it receives...and you will enjoy those special memories. Now, tomorrow and forevermore...

Happy Valentine's Day...

February 13, 2011

"WHEN YOU DISCOVER LOVE, LIFE BEGINS"

When life begins for each of us we are only living on instincts. Soon we learn to appreciate life and those things and people around us. Then "when you discover love, life begins" to bring you living memories that last you into eternity...

Love adds meaning to all that you are. How you approach love will determine how others think of you. How you accept love will build your character and endear you to others forevermore. One day "when you discover love, life begins" to enrich you with each heart that you touch...

"When you discover love, life begins" to fulfill your dreams while giving you those treasured memories. Life begins to deliver you the blessings from Heaven and all that life has to offer you. "When you discover love, life begins" to be simply the joyous reward that your heart continuously longs for...

November 6, 2010

INSPIRATION

"We change our relationships with others when it becomes necessary to gather all of what we are to focus on having peace of mind"...

"The successes of the best should increase the efforts of those seeking to be the best"...

"A BUILDING BLOCK IN THE HOUSE OF HOPE"

When one needs, one finds solutions for those needs and that's how Black Americans became Americans. Little did each know they were "a building block in the house of hope"...

On a long and dark night he got the call and made the historical ride shouting the alarm, "the British are coming", yes Paul was "a building block in the house of hope"...

Tall and lean he stood pondering the issues that troubled his mind. Men were dying, the country was divided and stuck in the middle were many souls which continued to be wronged. In the end a great document became a beacon of hope for those wronged souls. Abe wrote the Emancipation Proclamation, "a building block in the house of hope"...

There are many building blocks in the history of our land. Most are not famous...some are not known. I hope they all knew they were "a building block in the house of hope"...

The latest famous one has a strange name for an American, Barack Obama... the President elect in 2008, "a building block in the house of hope". He has shown us that the American dream is real...so try my friends and each of you can...be "a building block in the house of hope"...

November 08, 2008

"A PEACEFUL NIGHT"

All day long your life is visible to those around you...you laugh, they know it. You talk and they hear you. You move and they see you. Oh, how we all wish for "a peaceful night"...

In a loving relationship there is much to do, and even more to live with. Your emotions drive you, as the emotions of those you love drive them in a similar way. Compromising is what we do. Yes, it is better now! As the lights go out we pray for "a peaceful night"...

Lying flat in this fox hole is not fun. I want to stand or sit really bad. Living is more important to me so I just lay here turning to and fro as the evening sun sinks low. The cover of night is near, I know I can move more freely then. Soon I will sleep so I pray, Lord, let it be "a peaceful night"...

"A peaceful night" we all do want, hope for and even dream of sometimes. If life is truly that drab, don't go to bed mad the experts say. Forget about work, relax your mind. For no matter whom you are or what life brings your way, it is all made better with "a peaceful night"...

November 16, 2008

"ACHE IF YOU MUST, BUT KEEP ME STRONG"

There are tears to shed...for what life has brought for me to bear...and they are tears of sorrow. Yes they came, but my tears of joy...will I remember forever-more. To my eyes I say, if you must shed tears...may they be tears of joy for the worst is past and gone...

How I tremble, shutter and even shake when the negative thoughts attempt to conquer my conscious thinking. The Lord has blessed me with mental strength which holds my focus on the positives of...living beyond the stormy times. Mind, if you must think, make the negative thoughts become building stones...of the paved path I faithfully follow into the future...

Oh Lord you know my heart is aching...my soul is sorrowful...and I am in pain...so Lord, God hear my prayer. Heart, "ache if you must, but keep me strong"...continue to pump hope to my mind...when negativity tries to make me weak. Send joy through my veins to keep me strong so my tears are joyous... for that which was bad has passed and gone. Let me be the person others know me to be. Lord as I pray, I thank you for showing me the way...and getting me thru another day...for keeping me strong so I can carry on. Heart, "ache if you must, but keep me strong", for there are many that need me...to help them carry on...

July 5, 2008

"ALONE ON A LONG ROAD HOME"

I'm out here living my dream. Now that I am deeply living my dream, I realize that there are issues that I did not dream of...and I don't know if I will survive. I am just an old man in the sea with a fish too large to get into my boat. Lord, I am "alone on a long road home" please...take care of me...

I was raised on a small farm and learned to live off the land. Back when I was young, I was married with a child. The Union Jacks tortured and killed all that I loved...and left me to die too. I survived and became their worst nightmare for many years. I have fought and killed until I am lost in being "The Outlaw Josey Wales". I am "alone on a long road home" Lord, teach me to love again...

These are stories that may or may not be true, but they are examples of what life can present you. Be it a dream gone wrong or a tragic event in your life, at some point you will be "alone on a long road home". Remember that you are never alone...for God is always there with you...

If you are traveling back home from fear, an addiction, an accident, a broken heart, a lost loved one or any other troubling issues...just remember to pray. Then when God's Angels reach out to you, just relax and allow them to guide and comfort you...when you are "alone on a long road home"...

January 1, 2010

"THE BIRTH OF MY TOMORROWS"

I woke and was feeling about the same as each day before. I became aware that all of my senses were still with me, thank God for that. It is a new day in my life so how great of a day can I make it for myself? As it comes to me that it is my birthday, I smile and I reflect back to my yesterdays. It occurs to me that "the birth of my tomorrows", must start today...

When I awake tomorrow and each tomorrow to come, I must have the will to wake day after day. What can I do today to make me excited when I awake tomorrow, remembering yesterday. Can I give my best today so I have no regrets tomorrow, if all did not go my way? Can I see the best in me in the mirror as I stare back at myself? That only happens if I am all so proud of me. Can I find comfort for my soul within me? One can never truly mask a troubled mind and soul. Truthfully, this moment is "the birth of my tomorrows" and I must cry out so that others know I am reborn...

Physically, we can only be born once and that is the greatest day of our lives, for we have not sinned, hurt anyone, taken advantage of any situation or disappointed others or ourselves. Each day that follows brings the opportunity for all of that. "The birth of my tomorrows" will define me, for as others evaluate their daily birth, many will be affected by mine. Will I give as much love as I demand for me? Will I trust others and will they feel that they can trust me? Will I be able to give the gift of forgiveness, for it is the greatest gift I can receive...

Can I be patient enough for others to show their greatness to me? Will I have the compassion that I so often desire? Will I dream of tomorrow being greater than today? That can only happen if I did not fail me on yesterday. "The birth of my tomorrows" starts with me, my every thought, my every action, my every desire, even my every dream. Awake just as a child just born and cry out...this is "the birth of my tomorrows" and I will be proud to be born again and again...on each tomorrow to come...

August 20, 2011

"BLOCKS TO THE GOLD"

Who can achieve that which is not desired? How do you win if starting is not important? How can you do your best when you do not know there is a need to do your best? Winning requires you to get from the "blocks to the gold"...

An undeveloped plan has no true objective to achieve. A poorly planned journey is more difficult to make. Once side tracked, achieving a goal requires a greater effort. Traveling from the "blocks to the gold" is important in all of life's journeys...

Place your successes on a block of hope...then have the faith to move from one block to the next. Push off each block to gain the advantage that you need...then push harder to separate you from negativity....while ignoring that which you have no control of. Mostly, believe in yourself, for life requires your best...as you journey from the "blocks to the gold"...

August 05, 2008

"BUILDING YOUR DREAM"

Dreaming is a blessing which is like a wish...but only better. Dreams can become reality, if you work to make them come true. Wishes are only thoughts, which if they come true...only please you. Dream, then visualize "building your dream"...

Start by clearing the way that is necessary for you to build the dream. Chop down all obstacles and remove all doubts...so you have a level plane to start the building process. It is then that the plan has a chance and you can begin "building your dream"...

Establish a solid foundation...by understanding what it takes to build. For without understanding, confusion and doubt will creep in and...your foundation will not support your dream...

A structure of hope gives you a reason to keep building and allows you to know where you are and...that the building is going well. With hope resting on understanding...the possibility of success is there...and now others see that you are "building your dream"...

With an exterior and a roof of faith...the possibilities are endless. No step ever ends with despair...for faith shows you the way to go. A surrounding of faith forms an environment of success...now you are almost finished with "building your dream"...

When the interior is finished with goodness and furnished with joy...all want to enter to be a part of your dream. Let goodness welcome them in...while joy shows them that they are appreciated. It is then that you know that "building your dream" is priceless because...of what it took to build and how others admire it...

January 31, 2009

"BURIED TREASURES ARE WASTED BLESSINGS"

Watching and doing nothing is a common way of living. Politicians do it...for it is more important to be politically correct. They have the talent and power to make the difference...yet they don't. Their "buried treasures are wasted blessings"...

A child is born and then the mother is left alone...to raise the child, while the father moves on to the next woman...to do it again. He's using the knowledge, charm and efforts given by God so he can be a provider...in the wrong way. His "buried treasures are wasted blessings"...

It is sad that "buried treasures are wasted blessings" day after day in most of our lives. We prepare to assist but assist not...we prepared to act but take no action...we learn and learn but fail to teach...then we preach and pray to each other...while sin grows out of control. That's not living...our "buried treasures are wasted blessings"...

Uncover your treasures...to enjoy your blessings. Stand for right for wrong is never right. Help those in need to make what you have your treasure. Learn so that you can teach...others to find their treasures. For a life in which "buried treasures are wasted blessings", is like being a desolate island...in the sea of life...

September 7, 2008

"BURY DESPAIR TO MAKE ROOM FOR JOY"

Death is a constant reminder that life continues to change for each of us. We live knowing that we will not live forever. For all will die someday, leaving the world we know in hopes of spending eternity in Heaven. By ending life on earth you "bury despair to make room for joy" in Heaven...

No one makes perfect decisions all of the time. We all take a wrong path from time to time, ending up in situations which are just not good. They make life uncomfortable and create the need to decide you need a change. Have the strength to endure the change and have faith that the change will bring a better tomorrow. You must "bury despair to make room for joy" in the tomorrows to come...

Despair comes to those who choose to allow negativity to control their thoughts. Those not willing to let go of the bad things or choosing to love that which they cannot have or don't need. Those that are blinded by their wants as they constantly ignore their needs. You must understand the need to "bury despair to make room for joy" in your live...

Joy is achieved, no, it is not a given! Joy is there within you just needing you to give it a chance to be significant in your life. Joy overwhelms you positively, if you just live to achieve it. Joy is what makes life worth living. Joy overshadows hurt, pain and even despair. If you let it, joy will comfort you. So have your mind take control of your heart...for it knows to "bury despair to make room for joy" in your heart...

January 18, 2009

"CHARACTER GROWS FROM WITHIN"

We all start about the same way. A slap on the butt and we cry out. Then all know the child is born...the child is alive. At that age the child don't know that "character grows from within"...

Minutes become hours, which become days, to add up to months...for we record age in years. Others must care for the child as it grows...nourishing the body and the soul. Somewhere within, the child begins to learn, develop and understand. These are critical years in a child's life...for "character grows from within"...

Now having a mind of your own, life becomes more difficult to live. Decisions you have to make, paths in life you must decide to take. There are feelings now and all are not good. Some you wish to change, others you hate to lose. Experience is what you are gaining now...a key factor in whom and what you become. For living is what lets you know "character grows from within"...

Take it all in and then sort it well...dispel the bad...cling to the good. Pray for understanding while believing faithfully in God. Bring joy to your soul by... having hope for tomorrow. So when your "character grows from within", it will be character that pleases and...causes others to love you as a friend...

February 22, 2009

"DISCOVER YOU IN A ROOM FULL OF STRANGERS"

Comfort is desired by all at all times. For it is comfort which allows you to relax, feel special, safe and cared for. Some refer to it as a zone, yet others only feel it at home. Try to "discover you in a room full of Strangers" to know who you are...

Our military teaches how to be warriors with strength, honor, brotherhood and commitment to duty. Warriors must overcome the elements before...they overcome you. Warriors never leave a fallen brother behind. Warriors plan for the worst then fight to live...not just win. Warrior, if you are captured just "discover you in a room full of strangers"...and never give in...

On a plane you sit alone with others you don't know. Maybe you chat or just focus on your own mission. Sometimes others invade your space or disrespect your wish...to be left alone. You know not their situation and probably don't care...but it is a prime time...to "discover you in a room full of strangers"...

Do I posses patience, do I really care? Am I willing to give some of my time?

Will I entertain the issues of others...with an attentive ear? Is my time too precious to share? Can I expand my world to accept...one person more? Can I deliver others...when danger is near? Have I the strength to...help others in need? Do I have the compassion to hold...another's hope in my hands? Only you know if you "discover you in a room full of strangers" ...that know not who you are...

December 19, 2009

"DON'T FEEL THE PRESSURE, CREATE IT"

Objects that are left unprotected can become a target for others to take. Hearts which are open for others to use, get used and...left to be mended by others...

The years of none productive activities...are just wasted times. The worker that doesn't see the way to produce...starts to feel the pressure of failure and then...the fear of not surviving...

The fish that is unaware of the hook, like the prey that is unaware of the hunter...will soon feel the pressure of fear...then death...

The pressure is always waiting to get the upper hand on you man. There is no escaping this in your life. So you must defend yourself and that is only done by becoming...the pressure that overwhelms the pressure which seeks to attack you. Simply said "don't feel the pressure, create it" instead...

October 17, 2007

"DON'T JUST SHINE, BRING WARMTH TO THE WORLD"

Be more than a man...be a father and a mentor...to lead the young through their more difficult years...

Be more than a woman...be a mother and a lady...that teaches the young how to find their place in life...

Be a friend that is always there...listening, caring and sharing all that you have...

Be a lover and not just a partner and bring joy to your loved one...by being a truly loving soul...

Be a teacher that gives more than knowledge by bringing life to your teaching...for it shows that you care...

Be more than a learner be an inquiring mind...that thirsts for learning how to live...

Be more than a hero or celebrity...be the inspiration for others by showing...

how real life is to be lived...

So don't just show who you are and what you have...show what you have in your heart as well and create positive paths for others to follow...

So be what God intended you to be...for when God's Angels speak...they say, "don't just shine, bring warmth to the world"...

June 28, 2008

"ENJOY THE SUNSHINE, RAIN IS NATURE'S DRUMBEAT"

We wake in hope of seeing the sunshine and feeling the heat that comforts us on those chilly mornings. Oh how a nice calm day excites us...for we can, "enjoy the sunshine, rain is nature's drumbeat"...

Often that promise of a nice and calm day is broken...for we awaken to a rainy or stormy day. We see the rainy days in a negative way... because we do not understand nature's way. Take the time to "enjoy the sunshine, rain is nature's drumbeat"...

As the rain drops fall...so do our hopes of enjoying the sunshine...but the enjoyment of sunshine should always be a memory...if you have enjoyed it well. The rain drops fall as they will or may and no one or nothing can escape nature's skills. Those drops you feel if you are exposed to them...you see if you are not concealed from them...and you smell if you are not isolated from them. In a way, they are like the sunshine...so "enjoy the sunshine, rain is nature's drumbeat"...

All of God's creatures can enjoy the rain and you are a lucky man...if you recognize that rain is nature's drumbeat. Watch how the animals and fowls rise...to dance to those drumbeats. Listen to them applaud...as nature plays. You should feel the warmth of the drumbeat...just like it is sunshine. Learn to experience the fragrance that only those with keen senses...know how to appreciate. Just taste a droplet...and you will want more. Be thankful, "enjoy the sunshine, rain is nature's drumbeat"...

When I say "enjoy the sunshine, rain is nature's drumbeat", you may not understand just what I mean. Try standing in a dusty desert where rain seldom falls...watching how God's creatures fight for each droplet as they fall. Listen to the farmers' prayers...when no rain comes, for sunshine is not enough...for what they grow. In case you don't know or recognize how...nature's drumbeat is...what makes everything grow...

October 5, 2008

"FAITH, COURAGE AND WANT"

The unknown is always challenging to anyone. Through faith we are able to know what was unknown, but faith alone is never enough...

One must have the courage to try...in order to succeed. One must have the courage to keep trying...when failure seems to be the only answer...

Keep in mind courage is only a word...till one wants to dream first, then succeed. One must want to achieve or one just settles for doing...that which the faithful, courageous "want to bees" don't want to do...

Have faith and courage to achieve...what you want to accomplish in your lifetime...

December 1, 2008

"FLY HIGHER THAN EAGLES"

In the mirror, I see my beauty and so much more. You can shop a lifetime and never posses what I have. I live to someday have golden slippers whose reflection can be seen in these green alluring eyes of mine. My curly locks frame my naturally beautiful face, like a crown that a queen deserves. During my younger years I wanted to "fly higher than eagles" to never lose sight of how wonderful life can truly become...

Life speeds on so I always have to do my best to keep pace. I am a Florida girl and I wear purple for it represents the passion in me. Pink is my favorite color for it represents the survivor in me. I have loved and lost that love, yet I am blessed with a most joyous gift of a daughter that I love unconditionally. I have survived great challenges in my life, for family and friends are always there supporting me. My tribute to them is my wings that you can see, only if I share them with thee. With them beneath my wings, I "fly higher than eagles" and the world I see keeps inspiring me...

Come help me grow my wings so I can shelter those that have no wings of their own. I need to carry some to higher places so fear, deceit and despair cannot clip their wings. I must cover some so that the coldness of condemnation doesn't put out their eternal flame. I "fly higher than eagles" for my inner strength keep lifting me, showing others that it can be achieved...

November 19, 2011

"FOR"

For all the years that you did not get it right...know that the opportunity to get it right never disappears...if you never give up trying...

For the special moments that you shared to only be over shadowed by moments you want to forget...know that new great moments are always possible...if the great memories are relived...

For the years lived struggling in so many ways...know that your struggles were not in vane...if you made the best of what you had...and you are a better person today...

For now is the new beginning...a new day...for you have the opportunity to right the wrongs of yesterday. You are the key to your happiness...not others. So let not you make you unhappy...for happiness is in your mind...for your heart to find...and enjoy while you live...

October 25, 2007

"FOR TOMORROW TO BE"

Today must be lived "for tomorrow to be"...to be joyful, enjoyable and mostly...to be memorable...

Today must be seen "for tomorrow to be" visualized. Visualized as an improvement of yesterday, as a day to remember, as a day I made a difference... and as the beginning of a better me...

Today must be forgotten "for tomorrow to be" a new beginning...beginning to right yesterday's wrongs... beginning a path to ensure a better tomorrow... and the beginning of a more understanding me...

Today must pass "for tomorrow to be" coming...coming with renewed hope...with stronger faith...with a better way of living and...with love that is everlasting as well as forgiving...

"For tomorrow to be" I must change...change for the better...to keep improving for tomorrow...to improve what I have become. I must change...for tomorrow will be today...when tomorrow comes...

July 12, 2007

Stephen McDonald

"FROM DUST TO DAWN"

Man works for many reasons....some are related to the basic need to survive...whereas others are related to what one wants. Man must work "from dust to dawn"...

Life begins the same way for all mankind and life ends...the same for all mankind as well. The quality of one's life is dependent on...how one lives "from dust to dawn"...If dust is the beginning then dawn is the end... yes death awaits us all...

Dust is the beginning of one's understanding of life and dawn is...the end of living one's legacy of life...yet, dawn is also the beginning of eternity. Only you are responsible for how...you live "from dust to dawn" so live it right, live it well...choose eternity and not hell...

Live a life that brings you joy...allows you to not only dream but live those dreams...allows you to have the faith to believe not only in you...but in God as well. Live a life that finds you loving as you are loved. You must learn to truly live "from dust to dawn"...for when dawn comes...you will be judged on how you lived...and there will be no changing...the eternity for your soul...

September 14, 2008

"FROM THE OCEAN TO THE TWIN PITONS"

We may not be an old country but our land has been here almost forever. One day it claimed itself from the sea and the Twin Pitons have been a beacon to us every since. We have always loved our land and it has always provided us with so much more than just life. "From the ocean to the Twin Pitons" life is lived freely on each joyous day...

Often there are many visitors and even some that we don't desire. Our heritage let all know what we are about. The Land, The People, The Light are endless treasures that each of us adore. This "Helen of the West" we will fight always to protect and to preserve. Tomas, you attacked us "from the ocean to the Twin Pitons". We may be battered and hurt, yet I can still lift my eyes to adore my St. Lucia from the ocean shores to the heights of the beloved Twin Pitons. World, listen to our voices as we declare our National Pledge for our spirits can never be broken...

Our flag still flies and our spirits keep us standing strong and together to

98

match the strength of our home land. We have a will to be better and that always drives us to achieve. We trust in God and that always gives us hope. We act responsibly and that earns us your trust. So as we live we will rebuild "from the ocean to the Twin Pitons". Give us a little time and then come celebrate and relax your mind...

November 2, 2010

"GIVE YOUR LIFE A CHANCE TO BE AN ADVENTURE"

In the shadows of others is an okay place to be. Being there may be comforting, but it is also limiting you. Let the sunshine light up your world and see what is there for you to gain...

When you approach a road you have not traveled, you always wonder what is to be seen or known if you just travel that road. All roads lead to something. It may be something that is missing in your life...

Meeting new people is welcomed by so many, yet many prefer to shy away from the people they don't know. Their comfort zone is all they want to experience. The world changes because people step outside their comfort zones to ask what if and then do what they want to experience...

Loving relationships are often ended because one fears rejection or that the relationship will not work out or last forever. Forever is undefined, now is real. Passing up love is time lost loving and time that cannot be recovered...

When faced with the opportunity, "give your life a chance to be an adventure". Take a chance and travel that unknown road. Step out of the shadow and feel the sunshine. Meet new people and experience life through them. Let your loving relationships grow, knowing you are strong enough to survive what you fear...

"Give your life a chance to be an adventure". Walk with God having hope and taking leaps of faith. Learn what awaits you in adventures you have not lived...

July 27, 2008

"GO ON, DREAM BIG THEN ACHIEVE"

I look into the eyes of the successful people. There I see the excitement like that of a child. Setbacks are a constant reminder of just what it takes to be successful...So if you are thinking small "go on, dream big then achieve"...

In one's latter years there are battle scars which hopefully are over shadowed by victories of many sorts. It is easy to tell that the old know their greatest accomplishments are behind them, accomplished in their younger days. If asked they would tell you "go on, dream big then achieve"...

There are no rules for dreaming. In fact it is an act that none of us can control. Dreams come to you in your sleep for they are thoughts of those daring to entertain changing their lives. "Go on, dream big then achieve" your dreams...

Make the stars an image in the rearview mirror of your memory. Look down at the highest mountain peaks from your perch up above. Drown out the voices of many with your calming voice of reason. Let your bar of achievement be the bar you set and the bar others want to get up to "go on, dream big then achieve" what only you can dream and later celebrate when you have achieved...

November 16, 2008

"GROW MORE YOURSELF"

As their little eyes look at you...please see more than the sparkles...see what they want to see in you. Then help them see...and "grow more yourself"...

Their little ears are ready to hear of yesterday and the days to come. Provide them with stories both good and bad...for this is how they learn...and you "grow more yourself"...

Their little hands work feverously to solve that which they desire to know... yet the right solution they may not find...so just take their hands and walk them through that door. Then another world they will know and you get the chance...to "grow more yourself"...

The means of growing all should want to know and explore...forevermore. The art of how to grow many of us know...for us...life is just living...if that is all that you do. So share what you have learned...and "grow more yourself". For it is only through sharing knowledge that one knows...the secret to acquiring knowledge is...to "grow more yourself"...

July 19, 2008

"HAVE A FEELING OF YOUR OWN"

Was it really necessary to copy what the Joneses did and was it not possible to have your own dream...was your world that upside down or...was the pain just too much to bear...

Was the stars not aligned with your sign and was the sun so hot it dulled your mind. Was it the wrong day of the week...or were you sick or too tired to think. Was it just not inside of you...please tell me if there wasn't anything that was going your way...

My friend...here is what I must say to you...learn to have a great time on your own and have your own thoughts...that lead you day by day. Mostly, pray and keep the faith forevermore. Life should then change for you and...allow you to "have a feeling of your own"...

October 17, 2007

"HAVE YOU THE TIME"

In the end when life is over for you there will be little time for you to make amends. In fact, you may not even know the time is near. Will it be okay to move on from those that you love and will comfort accompany you on your last journey of life...

In you, what did others see...what did others think of you? How far did they go to give you a helping hand? Who will miss you, and just tell me why. Who truly respects you and will promote your name...

Today and yesterday are lived already. So it is tomorrow that the changed you must live. So "have you the time" to search your soul, cleanse the wrong that you find, cultivate the good in you, find that path to a better you or just right your wrongs by being strong...

"Have you the time" to give of yourself, that which others need to find their way. "Have you the time" to live life right so that your life is a life worthwhile...

May 16, 2008

"HOW CAN I DREAM OF THE UNKNOWN"

I step as proudly as I can, but I have little to be proud of. Some see me and think that it is fear which appears to be overcoming me. It is not fear... it is just me trying to understand all that has happened to me. It drives me crazy, for so many keep asking why I did not do things that I never knew could be done. Tell me "how can I dream of the unknown" and make that dream come true...

I know the life I live like I know the back of my hand. I know there is other lives I can live as I know there is a back of my head, yet I know I can see neither without some help from something or someone else. The history of our land is important as is Math, English and knowledge of the Arts. The expectation is that I will dream of these and plan my life accordingly. Please understand that I live across the river from such expectations and I need a bridge to get across that river, for "how can I dream of the unknown" adventures that you hope I learn to live...

Please go beyond teaching me of things and places I have not heard of and therefore have no desire to have or visit. Instead teach me to appreciate myself and what I have to give to my life. Teach me of the greatness of God and how his Angles will protect me. Teach me to fear being ignorant so I have a greater desire to learn. Teach me of the blessing I can give to other, once I prove that they can trust me. Teach me that there is joy in knowing that better ways of living exist beyond the boundaries that my mind has imprisoned me behind. Please help me build that bridge across that river that emits that constant fog of despair, keeping me as I now am. "How can I dream of the unknown" or have hope that I will ever be more than...my fear within will ever allow me to imagine for me...

April 2, 2011

"HOW MANY HEARTS DID YOU TOUCH"

Deep in the jungle, centuries ago they used the beat of the drums to let all know what was to happen in the moments to come. Children grew more excited as each beat sounded. The adults knew their roles and scenes were played out as a way of life. As life escaped the warrior's body with those he loved at his side, I hope the chief asked him "how many hearts did you touch"...

Great poets, writers and singers too, they perform, give and inspire yet most that admire them they never meet. Was their talents theirs or gifts that they could keep giving to those in need. I wonder if they were ever asked "how many hearts did you touch"...

Good fathers and mothers in all of the land do what is right and set the right examples too. Giving that which you have in a loving way to those that you love, know and yes, others too. For goodness should never be hidden, it should be there for all to see. For time after time it is on display right next to those showing the negative way. Shield it not in any way for one day you will not be able to provide it anymore. Then, when you are standing in Heaven as one of God's angels on call...you can ask other "how many hearts did you touch"...

March 01, 2009

"HURRICANE LIFE"

Yes, there are tears in my eyes, sadness in my every move and despair can be detected in my every word. The warning signs were there for me to see, to evaluate and then react to... appropriately. I ignored them all and now "hurricane life" is battering me...

As a child, the first warning signs were there. I kept going when told to stop and I refused to move when asked to act. It was more important to me to have my way than see the way to steer clear of the fierceness of "hurricane life"...

In school and college, I did just enough to achieve. Reserving my best for those things I wanted to do to please me. Lessons I should have learned were warning signs from those ships which survived "hurricane life". No, those ships did not appeal to me so I passed them thinking the cover of darkness would shield me. "Hurricane life" gladly welcomed me in...

As a professional, I knew I had arrived by freeing myself of the bonds of parents and teachers. I was warned of the pitfalls of selfishness, arrogant and told I could not do it alone. I was my own me in my own world. Let me tell you, ignore these warning signs and your safe passage through "hurricane life" will be gone...

"Hurricane life" has beaten and battered man all these years. Don't be foolish...heed the warning signs. Stay prepared to make it through...for you are in the eye of "hurricane life" and the second half of the storm of living...just isn't forgiving...

September 6, 2008

"I BUILT MYSELF"

I arrived on earth not alone which was good because I was not able to feed myself, but that did not stop me from being born. I had a will to live and a purpose for being alive. I grew continuously and it took a while to learn how to first crawl...then walk and...finally I could feed myself and even start to speak. I learned quickly that I had to build myself because others could do only so much and they...could never know exactly who I was and what I needed to grow myself...

I learned that which I saw, I touched, I smelled and mostly that which I heard. It all reinforced my need to build myself in a way to make me happy and proud. I went to school, but not alone...for in my head I had a dream with a working plan...a plan to win at the game of life. I truly knew the urgency...so "I built myself"...

I conquered the early years while others around me constantly failed. Now my success became the classroom tale that the other students loved so well...

I battled to not be known as just another nerd...so "I built myself" to fit in while unknowing to them...I just kept stacking more blocks to build me stronger...

I faced great struggles to stay focused, to fit in...and live within the blocks that I built me from. Others wanted me in their arms...but the arms I loved was those of my mom and family. I grew stronger, wiser and more aware. Then one day it all came clear and I knew from where my plan came...why I understood so much more...than most of those my age. I discovered mom was still building herself...just ahead of me. Now I could see why she was so pleased with me...

I cannot wait to build me more...since my adult days have changed my needs... my building blocks are more serious now...yet my plan is still working just fine. You may not like who I am...or you may see me as too proud...but my building plan anticipated such actions...and it does not affect my plan for I know who I am...because "I built myself"...

August 7, 2007

"I CRASHED BUT I DID NOT BURN"

Looking back and thinking about my life thus far, I have great joy in knowing how I got to where I am. Joy does not come without some complications and even some failures. "I crashed but I did not burn"...

I have related to many people during my lifetime, had the love of many and loved many too. I have crushed the dreams of some that wanted me for a lover and yes, suffered when my dream for that special lover was shattered. Yes, "I crashed but I did not burn"...

I have no gold, platinum or black card that guarantees the world will be nice to me...and I know for certain you do not have one either. I have what it takes to overcome despair, conquer fears and reach for the stars of hope. Because I have this character...yesterday "I crashed but I did not burn"...

My goals are achieved because I will me to achieve them. I constantly set new goals so that...my achievements are not wasted dreams...and I constantly dream of being more tomorrow than I was yesterday. "I crashed but I did not burn" because my faith, dreams and desires always rescue me from...the fires of failure and the flames of despair...

August 24, 2008

"I HOLD A CLOUD"

I try to understand mankind and there is so much to know that my senses are confused. With fear overcoming me, I have little that I can do, so "I hold a cloud" in my full view for this cloud comforts me. In my cloud there is peace for only joy is in my heart. There is hope too, for a path appears before me. I need only to walk it, to journey to other places that comfort me...

"I hold a cloud" above all that I imagine for that cloud has energy that allows me to be all that others desire of me. When tomorrow is here, that cloud will continue to reveal my secrets that others seek to know...

"I hold a cloud" within my world for that cloud reminds me that each day is not given without challenges to conquer. Each day is lived within that cloud, filled with my dreams of tomorrow and made more colorful by my memories of yesterday...

"I hold a cloud", a cloud of certainty and imagination that opens each day to shower my life with excitement, joy and renewed hope. Oh, how wonderful to-morrow can become, if "I hold a cloud" that allows me to live life freely today...

October 16, 2011

"I JOURNEY ON"

When others think of me, they may wonder how I came to be as I am and why I stay that way. "I journey on" not just for me, for there is a much greater need than I could ever desire. Those that are wondering...it is ironic, but they need me to be...the me that they see...

"I journey on" for the family that I cherish, for the unspoken yet constant confirmation that I am loved, for the promise that on tomorrow, we will live more special memories and because I have faith that God will always deliver me...

"I journey on" for I still dream and there must be a tomorrow to live those dreams, for I am a conqueror and there are challenges that still haunt me, for there are adventures that I can only experience in my soul, if it is focused on how I dream tomorrow to be and because of the chance that I can make tomorrow more special than yesterday...

My imagination of years past started the journey that I am on. Change is a constant and I guess that is what makes life an adventure. This change is no different from all of the rest, so "I journey on" for all that I am and all that I care for is constantly driving me to keep the faith with each step that I take. I have my family and great memories to comfort me as "I journey on"...

September 25, 2011

"I NEED TOMORROW"

I look at my reflection in the mirror and I see the real me that only I know. Those many years of loving, hurting and joyous moments flash through my mind, telling the story of my life just like a movie script. "I need tomorrow" so I can live those most joyous moments over and over again...

Memories will always be with me, so I must sort through them and throw out the old baggage to make room for new memories I am destined to live. "I need tomorrow" to live and play out the script I dreamed last night...

Each new day brings the opportunity to make me more special to others. I only need to be my best to have no regrets when I remember my yesterday. I must love, be joyful and hope that others will love me. I must be faithful and give my gifts of caring and forgiveness unconditionally. "I need tomorrow" to prove I have gotten better than I was yesterday...

"I need tomorrow" to bring me renewed hope and to give the world a chance to witness all that I am. "I need tomorrow" to dream of a future of tomorrows filled with sunshine and those memorable sunsets that I watch with the one I love. "I need tomorrow" for I need a reason to dream then live those dreams joyously when tomorrow comes...

November 23, 2011

"I TAUGHT THE STARS TO SHINE"

Twinkle, twinkle little star is not just a childhood song, but also the beginning of a leading light to show others the way. I learned to twinkle too...and then "I taught the stars to shine"...

Apply yourself all parents, teachers and even the boss would say...you will need to shine one day...for one of tomorrow's leaders you must be. So I did as I was told and that made me want it even more...so I worked daily...and "I taught the stars to shine"...

Time and life coupled with my desires prepared me well. The grace of God was always there lighting...the right path for me to follow. I know my life's mission and I work day after day to succeed, to prepare then...give what money and precious items cannot satisfy. You see "I taught the stars to shine"...

My life would be empty if I leave nothing for the future leaders to build on... so I walk the path of success keeping God first. I give of my knowledge and I share it all in a loving way...so when I am gone to Heaven I will be able to say "I taught the stars to shine"...

June 28, 2008

"I WEAR A SMILE"

When you look at me it is happiness that I want you to see. You see happiness is rewarding me as well as you. For with happiness comes not only a smile, but much more...

Happiness brings others joy...because we love to share happiness. Happiness gives hope too, for the sight of happiness gives...hope for other in need of joy...

Happiness lets you know I'm alright this day. No forced smiles will I mask my face with this day...

Happiness is a celebration of the soul...and that smile lets all know that you are joyous. Joy brings me happiness that relaxes my face and that smile I wear... is the way I share joy with you...

January 20, 2008

"I WILL WAIT"

Some stand ready to be named, identified or placed on a pedestal for all to see. Time spent becoming what others want you to be is time some believe in spending of that which they cannot replace. Time passes and it waits not for thee...

It is often that one accepts that which is not right for them and the heart-aches they live with till they die. They will tell you that they must do it to be right, accepted or loved. My friend, true love only resides in the happy heart...

"I will wait" till I earn that which I desire to possess. Until my life's work earns me the recognition I desire. Until the way I live utilizes the time I have to live life the way it is suppose to be lived and until my lover has a happy heart just like mine...

"I will wait" on the Lord to touch my soul, point me to the right path of life and provide me all that I desire, For he makes me able to have, share and enjoy with others, the happiness in that endless love within me...

July 31, 2008

"IF THE MOUNTAIN BLOCKS YOU, IT'S YOUR FAULT"

Every Sizable stream or river was once just a trickle of water...flowing as gravity guides and pulls it toward the ocean. The water never stops seeking the ocean and there is a lesson for us all in this...if we can just understand it...

That water's journey is not easy for many factors, even the mountains...try to keep it from flowing to reach the ocean. That ole water it keeps on trying...for its destiny is its only mission and...anything less just will not do...

"If the mountain blocks you, it's your fault" for the answer is always there to be discovered...the path is there to be found. Yes, you will lose some of that which you love along the way...this will happen every day. The forest of despair will grow up around you...making your path harder to find. The clouds of disappointment will grow to fill the sky...to block your view of the stars...while the depth of the pitfalls keeps eroding...deeper with each new day. Meanwhile, treachery is all around you like a cloud of dust...trying to take your breath away...

Just remember your faith will lead the way...and give you hope when you need it most. If you keep standing...you cannot fall down. If the mind is willing...the body becomes able...so "if the mountain blocks you, it's your fault"... for not trying hard enough...to journey all the way...

November 1, 2008

"IF TIME STOOD STILL"

If you are looking into your soul, reflecting on your past and thinking of what you are doing right now...would you be proud of you "if time stood still"...

A frozen moment in time is usually a memory you want to relive over and over. What frozen moment of your life would do for you..."if time stood still"...

Sharing your life with the ones you love is such a wonderful feeling because of the laughing, sharing, giving and receiving. "If time stood still" are you with the persons...you desire to hold dear forevermore...

Life is a journey down a path similar to all others that you know, but it is your path...to walk and live on your own. "If time stood still" is your path one you are happy for others to know you traveled...

Tomorrow is dreamed about on yesterday or today and your path traveled yesterday...you can no longer change. Would you be excited about the steps you are taking and the path you are making...for tomorrow's journey..."If time stood still"...

"If time stood still" you could not change a thing in your life...so are you ready for life to end for you. "If time stood still" would you be satisfied and proud of...how others may remember thee. Just think "if time stood still" you would be exactly the person...others see and have to remember when they think of thee...

July 20, 2008

"IF YOU THINK YOUR HEART IS FULL"

Being fed up with what you are going through happens to all of us. Frustration sets in and that comfort you normally feel seems to escape through the pores of your skin. Relax your body and allow your mind to think. Hold your reactions just a little while longer. "If you think your heart is full" take control of you to discover there is room to allow comfort within...

Those around you will test you at times, demanding your time, material things and sometimes even more. They know not your true capabilities to give so they know not when to stop asking of you. "If you think your heart is full" just give some more to receive more to give...

People migrate to those that they trust and love for they seek that same level of peace within. A calming phrase or comforting touch is always what they need from you. "If you think your heart is full" help others find their peace and watch how much more peacefully you live...

"If you think your heart is full" you need only to provide some of what you have to others. That which you give or share will make your heart grow. It will leave room for more blessings and give you peace of mind. It will allow you to use the gifts God gave you to just give to those in need...

"If you think your heart is full", remember others gave their gifts to you...to make room in their hearts...to receive more gifts to give...

February 6, 2010

"I'M IN MY OWN WORLD"

I know what others may think of me...yet I am me and that pleases me...

I feel the stares, even those behind me...and it is that feeling that constantly drives me...

I hear the whispers and know they are about me...so I fuel my fire with them...so that they energize me...

I smell the air tainted with hate all around me...that air is cleansed by my love and joy...as it enters me...

I see the expressions they make when they look at me...secretly I think that those expressions...only highlight the beautiful me...

I taste the bitterness their snotty ways leave in the environment around me... fortunately, that bitter taste becomes sweet...when mixed with the compassion in me...

I am me, young, fine and beautiful. I'm so full of energy and not afraid to show it. I live for me and "I'm in my own world"...controlling who I let get close to me...

He who attempts to get in...enters hoping for what he feel he is missing. I am my world, the world that all can see...

April 26, 2008

"IN TRYING TIMES"

Your world is only great for you if you do what is necessary to make you happy, comfortable and yes content enough to have peace of mind...

Your world is just like our worlds, as fragile as a beautiful well crafted crystal vase that is desired by a chosen few. Yet, it is on display for all to see...

Your world can never be more than part of the world we live in and never better than the world around you allows it to become. Your world is lived "in trying times" just like mine...

"In trying times" your world cannot survive if it stands alone. The pressures of the world will crush your fragile world, leaving you in despair, leaving you wondering why and leaving you fighting to survive...

If you think you are so much better than we are, so great, too good or too fine to deal with the common many. If you think you are above the law or shielded by your wealth, then "in trying times" you will learn what is real...

"In trying times" when your world is shattered it will be that common many that is the world that shields you...and picks up your fragile pieces to rebuild your world. Alone, you are only in your own world...with the rest of us you are part of the world that remains united "in trying times"...

August 30, 2008

"INDEPENDENCE IN ME"

Living is not a dream...it is an adventure. An adventure one makes for one's self...because in you there is pride made possible by the inner you. I know there is "independence in me" for my adventure you all see...

Life is valuable to us all even if we do not live it well. Time is our greatest teacher and our character is the legacy of our life. Your character is what creates your adventure for others use your character as the main factor in deciding to share their adventure with you. Oh "independence in me", create that adventure to make others want to be with me...

My dreams have always inspired me and my character has always defined me. My hope has always encouraged me as my faith has always lifted me out of the valley of despair. My understanding has always endeared me to others. I have joy because of the "independence in me"...

The "independence in me" I hope you see...hope you understand and appreciate. For if it was not for the "independence in me"...you would not enjoy the adventure of knowing me...or the adventures you share with me...

January 25, 2009

"IS IT IN THE MIRROR OR IN THE HEART"

The secret to a good life is not an easy thing to discover...for the mind is always thinking and growing with every thought...and the heart is always working, yes even as we sleep...

Emotions they showed up one day. Maybe they were always there and we just discovered them one day. The mind and the heart they control them ole emotions...at lease it appears to work that way...

Together the three create the character we all have, hold dear...and try to understand in us as well as in others. Oh character, who am I really and why am I like I see me...when at times others see me differently...

The answer "is it in the mirror or in the heart"...do they know who and what I am, do I really show them me...or just a shadow to make them comfortable with me...

Is my character mine or just what others define as acceptable for me. Does my heart feel all that I am or...just feel what I think others want it to feel? The true image of me "is it in the mirror or in the heart" inside of me. It is only when the two are the same...that you can be proud of your name...

August 2, 2008

"IT'S MY POLE"

I look at it and let some others look at it too. Oh, the thoughts that must flood their minds when they see it for the first time. It is not just a stripper pole... my pole means so much more to me...like things which others don't know and cannot see or understand. Yea, "it's my pole" and it means so much more to me...than you are imagining it to be...

My pole is solidly anchored as I am solidly anchored to my family and my goals in life. My pole reaches for the sky and is symbolic with how I always will reach my goals. My pole is long and slender like a straight line, for my path to my goals requires a direct and definite commitment to achieve them. "It's my pole" do you understand now what it means to me...

As I climb my pole, my struggles of the past are relived each time my hands reach up for that next position, that position that gets me closer to my goals. I slip sometimes but that don't worry me for I am focused on overcoming the negatives in search of higher achievements...

"It's my pole" and it takes more than most are willing to try to climb to the top. I climb it with grace and confidence...and even a little showmanship. I am a pro at climbing and my achievements validate this. Think what you want of me, but understand "it's my pole"...the symbol of my struggles in life and...my goals to be achieved while living happily...

August 24, 2008

"JUST IN CASE"

"Just in case" you do not think yesterday was important, look at where you are today. Yesterday's lessons keep you from making mistakes today and yesterday's thoughts lead you to the dreams you have now. Yesterday's successes allow you to succeed today. I say yesterday was very important "just in case" you don't realize or recognize this at all...

A belt is worn with suspenders, "just in case" one of them is not enough. The mother brings extra diapers "just in case" the baby has an accident. The spare tire comes with the vehicle "just in case" you have a flat. God is always there "just in case" you are in need ...

Punting is part of football "just in case" the first down is not achieved. Overtime is part of sports "just in case" the outcome is not decided in regulation. Today is for correcting whatever "just in case" you did not get it right before.

Faith is important "just in case" you need hope for tomorrow...

Dream of eternity today, "just in case" your tomorrows never end. Your tomorrow is dependent on what you do today "just in case" you don't see it that way. Remember, today was dependent on yesterday when tomorrow comes...

You always have a gift to give "just in case"...someone is in need. Please recognize that forgiveness is your greatest gift "just in case"...you have the opportunity to give...

January 1, 2009

"JUST ROLL OVER THE POTHOLES"

The eyes are your windows to the world. Through them you see and that allows you to know so much more. You can see the best of others and maybe even your yesterday. You can see the roads you travel today and you can spot the troubling stretches of your life's journey. So "just roll over the potholes" to journey on in life...

You found yourself on the sad end of a loving relationship and know there were warning signs along the way. You ignored those signs and it is too late to turn around because the potholes are all around you. So "just roll over the potholes" you will live to love on better roads ahead...

"Just roll over the potholes" using the strength within you. You must adjust to the coming discomfort by creating flexibility in your every thought. Then re-stabilize from the shaky moments by faithfully moving on. You must remember these potholes for tomorrow they may still be there, just waiting to upset the normal you. If you slow your progress, you can avoid many of them; take the rest of them slowly, for that is the only way to minimize their impact on you...

In life you cannot go backwards and...you cannot sit still. Your future is before you just as...you dreamed of on yesterday. So one must "just roll over the potholes" to...cautiously travel on...dreaming of the tomorrows to come...

November 27, 2008

"KNOCK ON THE RIGHT DOOR"

Many doors look the same, be they falling in love or the way out of a bad relationship, the step to a successful future, an exit from a job you hate, the leap of faith to believe in God or your latest battle with the devil himself...

Doors are there for a reason. Some are to keep something secure, others keep something in whereas others keep the undesired out. Some are massive as others are frail, then some are works of art while others are just ugly...

As you work your way through the maze of living you will encounter many doors. What lies behind them is right and wrong...love and hate...success and failure...satisfaction and despair...hope and surrender...or faith and disbelief. So "knock on the right door" for...your prize of success is only behind the right ones....

All doors will not automatically open just because you are there. Peril awaits you on the other side of some that do. The maze of life is sometimes dark and dreary...causing you to look for shelter behind a friendly door. This is when so many doors look alike...and choosing the wrong one will bring you shame. It is important to protect your family name so always think and make sure. Then "knock on the right door" that leads you to the blessings...God hopes you find...

September 1, 2008

"KNOW YOUR ROAD HOME"

This time the opportunity may or may not prove to be what you want or need. I remember hearing the old fellows say as they discussed their troubling issues. In the end they would say...son, keep trying until you succeed...

The family tree is a tree like no other and every chip off the tree may not be good wood. Often the leaves under the tree did not fall from that tree. You might get shade but then you might get bird poop as well. So son, do what pleases you most...

All that you become aware of is not always what you need to have or know. All those that want to lead you may not know how to lead you through your chosen path in life. All that want you, surly they just want you for their own reasons...

"Know your road home" and travel it always. For on your road home, the curves do not surprise you and the trees tell you where you are. The position of the stars at night...is like a guiding light. The surface of the road you know well...so you can avoid the pitfalls along the way. Always "know your road home" and home...will never be more than a memory away...

July 29, 2008

"LEAP OVER THE STARS AND LEARN TO LIVE"

Great leaders like Mr. Douglas, Ms. Troutman, Dr. King, Ms. Parks and so many more...gave us visions and hope that encourages us on our journeys in life. You can too...if you "leap over the stars and learn to live"...

Your father and mother...most others will never know them as you do. Their guiding hand and loving hearts...helped make you what and who you are now. In summary they were teaching you to...just "leap over the stars and learn to live"...

Look under the wings of any superstar, actors, doctors, sportsmen or businessman...for basically they are all the same. A closer look shows that ordinary people that know...to "leap over the stars and learn to live"...are holding them up...

When so many try convincing me that stardom is what I should seek to have...I see the vision of my parents, Pastor and closest friends standing with God. I realize they are all I need...when they speak to me saying "leap over the stars and learn to live"...

Stardom brings attention and superficial comfort...whereas learning to live life...gives you peace of mind, direction, love and joy forevermore. "Leap over the stars and learn to live" with God as your guiding Star...

July 19, 2008

"LET EACH STEP BE BETTER THAN YOUR LAST"

From the moment you enter the world there are steps you must take to live a good life. The early ones are all instinctive. As you cling to the only love that you know and trust, you are taking positive steps. Be a survivor and "let each step be better than your last" as you grow strong...

The early years are what determine the life you will have as an adult. Learning is one of the most important steps. Loving is another key step that allows you to care. Being faithful is a step that helps you be joyful. "Let each step be better than the last" and your life will be enjoyable and rewarding as well...

As your steps become truer and your sight becomes more focused, your journey in life leaves a path you can always look back to see, analyze and plan to make the right steps tomorrow. Others can and will admire those paths which are rewarding. They have no desire to follow paths that lead to nowhere, or delay their decisions to make their next steps. So "let each step be better than your last" to be remembered forevermore...

Step truly, step proudly, and step faithfully...then step in good times or bad times...trusting that God is always with you. For when your time is all traveled...you will have but one step left to take. "Let each step be better than your last"...for your last step must last an eternity...

December 13, 2009

"LET THE TOP KEEP RISING"

For the fear of being less than you can be, "let the top keep rising". For the restlessness in your heart, "let the top keep rising". For those that mean the most to you, "let the top keep rising" for there is always room to grow and love more...

In those times when the world seems to be against you, "let the top keep rising". When you know your relationship with God is good, "let the top keep rising" for there is no limit to his blessings and grace...

Only when you try to achieve the most...can the top rise higher. So "let the top keep rising" for a top that never moves...never gets higher...and history tells that others' tops will rise above...that which does not move. So "let the top keep rising" in all that you do...

September 16, 2007

"LET'S ECHO SO OTHERS KNOW"

There are mountains in our lives that some cannot see, standing tall in the distance and seemingly unreachable. They could be a vision of tomorrow that we hoped for yesterday. "Let's echo so others know" there is higher ground and that the valley of despair will not last forevermore...

There are voices that we hear that so many cannot listen to. The voices whisper softly and sometimes they call our names. Mostly they guide us, bringing joy and comfort to us in our greatest time of need. "Let's echo so others know" those voices are trying to reach them too, before it is too late...

"Let's echo so others know" there is joy in living a good life. There is success when it is hoped for. There is knowledge when we listen to the voice of reason. There is soulful bliss when we have faith in God. There is great emotional bliss...when we love one another. It is important to know that there is an everlasting echo of your life when others remember you fondly...

"Let's echo so others know" though the path to heaven may not be easy... the path is joyous when you see the mountains and hear the voices...especially when you show others how to...see and hear them too...

September 27, 2008

"LIFE, IT'S ON YOU"

While others seek what they dream of, I must live as I dream. "Life, It's on you" to dream then live those dreams. Don't waste your dreams on things which make living harder than God meant for it to be...

When it is time to learn and gain wisdom, the window of opportunity continues to change. When you miss a lesson, other lessons may be harder to learn. "Life ,it's on you" to learn and gain wisdom or you will watch in frustration as life passes you by...for time waits on no one...

For beauty to be beheld, one must learn to appreciate all that God created for us to enjoy. Through the eyes, we behold beauty. Are you aware that the eyes only allow you to see it? Within us there are feelings which are the true judge of beauty. "Life, it's on you" to cultivate those feelings which allow the eyes to recognize all of the beauty around you...

Giving is a character that one has and we all have it within us somewhere. "Life, it's on you" to develop that character which allows you to give from the heart. Through faith and hope you find the joy to develop the skills to give. You see, giving is the best that you have to offer to others. "Life, it's on you" to live it well...

June 12, 2011

"LIFE'S STORMS WON'T STOP MY JOY"

Now that I control my life and must provide all that I need to live, I have discovered many ways to do that. Each day is mostly challenging and I understand the need to learn as I become victorious over each challenge. For tomorrow that knowledge will allow me to gain the victories I need to survive. "Life's storms won't stop my joy" for each victory allows me to journey into a new tomorrow...

As the voices of others create cloudy environments that make my challenges more difficult, I just find the silver lining in the cloudiness and use it as my shield and my armor. As their accusations rain down on my path and there is no shelter around, I find that my voice of reason and confidence in who I am are the best weapons to make sure "Life's storms won't stop my joy"...

I see their deceitfulness flashing before me like lightning bolts in a fierce storm. Just to be followed up by rumbling thundering consequences of their actions. With the confidence of David and the faith of Job I eventually prove to be the victor. For in my life journey God has prepared me so that "Life's storms won't stop my joy". Not today or on each tomorrow to come...

August 28, 2010

"LIVE AND ON POINT"

Viewing the streets of Ybor, provides one with so much to see and much more to ponder. The streets are filled with them, all types, shapes and colors. With each foot step there is an untold story. They walk to be seen and then walk some more to make sure that the world saw them. "Live and on point" they appear to be. Even in a group, they seek to be one lone thrill seeker, the star of the show...

It is like their hearts beat faster as the excitement overcomes them. Their costumes vary for they would not have it any other way. My favorite is the short skin tight dresses that seem shorter with their every step. I just smile as they tug to pull them back down for is shows they have some decency. Their footsteps should bring them back to reality; instead they just keep strutting, trying to be the star of the show. "Live and on point" they hunt excitement, that chance meeting or that special find...

It is ironic that they don't see it in themselves. Have they lost sight of the beauty that they work so hard to show, that very image they saw in the mirror just minutes before. Is it not comforting to just greet others by sharing a smile? Why all the drama, the shock factor and so much more. It is sad that they don't seem to live for themselves. "Live and on point" they move on without fear, without a true purpose that I can discern. I must wonder if they even have a true concept of time. The side walk jungle appears to sucks them in and it will until they learn to live, with the person within...

November 27, 2011

"LOOK BOTH WAYS, THEN PROCEED CAUTIOUSLY"

Man it is a shame that we do not use the lessons we learned in all situations we face. For each day as we walk our path of life we often say to ourselves "look both ways, then proceed cautiously" across the street, at the intersection while driving, even as we emerge into the hall at work...

Just think about the importance of this unconscious thought we have over and over again each day we live. Now apply it to other life situations and your life will be lived more joyously. Look at your pass, for life lessons were learned. Then look to your future to know where you are going. "Look both ways, then proceed cautiously" for happiness is a blessing...

The past has so much value that living today requires. Lessons learned, character you developed, knowledge you acquired, relationships you cherish... even having faith in God. Looking into tomorrow...is just planning your way... to give you a life to hope for as you dream of living your dreams. So just "look both ways, then proceed cautiously" the rest of your life. It will make your journey through life an adventure...to treasure for eternity...

May 10, 2009

"MAN, CHANGE YOU"

Lying awake at night because you have a troubled mind; man, that is not a good way to live...

Taking one more drink to busy yourself so that you do not have to face the realities of your life; man, there is no answer at the bottom of that glass...

Working on the less critical issues that you face while ignoring those that mean the most to you; man, those issues just won't go away just because you ignore them...

Man, stop praying that God will see you through while doing nothing to change the situation at hand; man, you must utilize the answers God give you to change anything in your life...

"Man, change you" and the issues you face, can't resolve or can't bear to think of will change as you do. Take charge of your life and "man, change you" to be a better you before the sun sets on thee...

July 26, 2008

"MORE CHAIN THAN YOU CAN SWIM WITH"

To understand what this means you have to visualize what it is. A chain is made of heavy metal links which weigh a lot. If attached to one's body, swimming is made more difficult. Then at some point the weight of the chain will sink you and all will be lost. Life is you and the way you live your life is the chain, so don't give yourself "more chain than you can swim with"...

Choices will always be presented to you. Which ones you make is all on you. Yes, you can allow others to make them for you if you want to live in their shadow and waste the true you. You need your own reference point to light your way, for each bad step you take in life forms another link in your chain. Remember if you have "more chain than you can swim with" you will sink like a rock...

God gave each of us the right amount of chain to swim through the treacherous waters of life. He made us able to swim with a little bit more, but he also gave us the ability to know when we have added too many links. He even gave us the tools to take some of the added links off our chain. God doesn't want you to have "more chain than you can swim with"...

Place the unwanted links of your chain on the anvil of understanding. Set your chisel of hope on the links you don't need and then swing your hammer of faith to break the unwanted links of chain. Then you will no longer have "more chain than you can swim with" and there will be joy and peace in your life. You can then swim your path through life's treacherous water using your reference point to guide you home...

January 10, 2009

"MY FOUR WALLS"

I am confined within four walls that are solid and strong. There is a floor there too that is often cold to the soles of my feet. I can look up and see my ceiling and know that somewhere above it...is freedom air. "My four walls" may confine me, but they will never conquer my soul...

I need only to close my eyes to take them out of my world. I need only to touch them to gain some of that strength that they posses. I feel how powerful they are and I know that my family is stronger still. You see, many loving hands built "my four walls" and I can feel those hands transferring some of their strength to me...

"My four walls" are built of materials very similar to those of my mother's home. Materials that ole Mother Earth made with her loving hands. Man may alter them, but they remain the same...similar to the love in a joyous soul. "My four walls" have their purpose and I have mine. For now we must reside together, but one of us knows that on some tomorrow, "my four walls" will not be in my life any more...

The cold floor will be replaced too, as soon as I walk through that last locked door. My ceiling will be bright and sunny days, which will be replaced by those star lit nights. Nights where my dreams will be more vivid, for they are not confined within "my four walls"...the den of hopelessness...

June 12, 2011

"MY LIGHT IS ALWAYS ON"

A ship is often all alone in the middle of the ocean. The horizon appears to be the same no matter which way you look. The captain depends on the sun or the stars at night to guide his way. He always knows that once close to home, the lighthouse will guide him the rest of the way. To the captain, the lighthouse keeper's most comforting words are "my light is always on"...

I live my life as all of us must. I feel joy and definitely know about pain. I cherish those I love and feel how they love me too. Happiness comes and sometimes it escapes me as well. I meet my challenges and I know I am not alone. For those that depend on me always know "my light is always on"...

Just walk a day in my shoes to understand how I came to be as I am. Come to me to find out how I love. Talk to me to understand the wisdom I have acquired. Look at me to know the confidence I possess. Touch me to know how comforting I can be. "My light is always on" and I pray that you too have...a light that others want to see...

September 27, 2009

"MY SMILE"

All of us want to be accepted by others, especially the ones we like a lot. Our eyes search in anticipation of that sign to let us know we are accepted by others. I submit to you my theory that "my smile" can tell you all you need to know about me...

"My smile" shows you the inner me that most never see. It is a reflection of how I feel about thee. It would not be there if there was no joy in me. If you caused "my smile" know that you are acceptable to me...For the rest of you, it is a blessing I give to you...for God gave it to me...

It takes a caring heart to smile genuinely. Look into the depths of my eyes to see the compassion and hope that are a great part of me. I want blame you if you touch me to see if my touch comforts you as much as "my smile". Just be warned that it may make you want to know more about me...

"My smile" is communicated so silently that often others don't realize what it says so loudly. See it as more than an acceptance of you or a simple polite greeting from me. See it as a beginning of you and me smiling together so happily because "my smile" is special to thee as yours is to me...

March 13, 2011

"MY STORY ENDS WITH A JOYOUS MOMENT"

I stood before the people and with the people and they found strength in me and gained hope with every word I spoke to them. I am famous for the words "I have a dream" and although I died at the hands of those hating me, "my story ends with a joyous moment" for today... so many are living my dream...

I felt the sting of the whips too. Oh how I cried from the pain, yet it drove me to believe in me. The dogs trailed me with the horsemen that were seeking me growing more angered as I eluded them. The souls with me prayed as I did and trusted my guidance in hope of regaining what should never have been taken from them. "My story ends with a joyous moment" for those souls...placed the soles of their feet on freedom soils...

"My story ends with a joyous moment" not because of who I am...but because of what I do. It is others that will tell the story about me one day...and the only story they can tell is the story they know. Lord, God I pray that "my story ends with a joyous moment" it matters not...that I do or do not know it. It just matters most that...the world knows forevermore...that "my story ends with a joyous moment"...

September 6, 2008

"NEVER LOSE YOUR IMAGINATION"

So much in life is not a given. Many fail to know this and their lives are full of disappointments. Therefore, one day they find that they don't know where they are or what they should be doing...

"Never lose your imagination" for you will lose so much more. You want be able to dream of tomorrow or see the beauty around you. You want be able to appreciate your journey thorough life for you will not be able to plan it...

Always pray for understanding for it helps you have hope for tomorrow. Then pray and ask for forgiveness even if you know not what you did wrong. It will also bring you joy and comfort which allows you to dream of your tomorrows to come. So "never lose your imagination" for that is the starter for your engine, the heart that drives you to become...

You must first imagine something to desire it. That is what causes you to dream it. Dreaming creates a greater desire which makes you take action to achieve. Just "never lose your imagination" and others will always define you as the amazing person you should imagine yourself to be...

August 08, 2010

"OLD BAGGAGE INSIDE"

I have a lot to live for and much to live to forget. Some things that were one time so special to me, they now only haunt me. "Old baggage inside" I feel you in me...

Times past brought me into this world and I enjoy life. I have experienced

124

the love of family and many more that did and still brings me joy. Then there are those experiences that brought me pain. "Old baggage inside" of me I know you, I know you too well...

Success is always hoped for. I hoped so for it that I gained what it took to achieve most of what I hoped for. Some of my decisions caused me pain and disappointment when I did not achieve to please me. "Old baggage inside" how do you manage to hang around so long...

"Old baggage inside" you can't hide and I can't hide you from the world so your existence is known by those that mean the most to me. You keep reminding me that you are inside me, in the heart where it matters the most...

Lord, God it is not freedom from this "old baggage inside" that I pray for you to give me...and no, I do not want to forget. God, just give me the strength to carry...this "old baggage inside" now, tomorrow and forevermore...

July 23, 2008

"ONE DAY AT A TIME"

The journey through life requires the best effort one can give. Many look for the secret code to life and get lost in a maze of wonderment, a deadly net cast by their own troubled mind. It would be best if they live life "one day at a time"...

I walk proudly through life today, for yesterday I prepared for my walk tomorrow. I will be comforted by all that I am and all of those special persons in my life. I waste no time trying to be famous, for I know that in living "one day at a time", my tomorrows to come will highlight my yesterdays and validate my importance to those I love , those I call mine...

I'm preparing me to keep living "one day at a time" for...I know that in living "One day at a time" I will enjoy all that God has in store for me, including all of the wonders that nature provides. I pray I am able to comfort those close to me and teach them...to live life "one day at a time"...

February 13, 2009

"ONE LONE SOLDIER, ARMY WHERE ARE YOU"

God created all things and the first man. There in the Garden of Eden man first lived well. Man was given woman, formed by God from one bone of man..."One lone soldier, army where are you"...

Man and woman proved they could not just be leader and protector of all, by being God's garden keepers. The story is told that it took just one bite of an apple from the Tree of Knowledge, the forbidden fruit..."one lone soldier, army where are you"...

Moses was born in trying times, protected by one who just did not know God's ways. As a young man he took a stand, then he took flight to save his soul, just to return to those he loved, to fight the greatest battle for his own... "one lone soldier, army where are you"...

He is one like no other that our country has known, a man well traveled, from a broken home. The waves of Hawaii he knows well. The fight of the common man is his battle ground. While the normal ones basted in their own brilliance, he worked in the shadows like those before him that history books have recorded. He is the modern day "Chosen One"..."one lone soldier, army where are you"...

I heard and saw that you needed me...so now I'm your President. I put your needs ahead of my desires...and I know my family is with me...as is so many more. I'm "one lone soldier, army where are you"...the world needs you too...

November 08, 2008

"OPEN YOUR WINDOW TO SEE THE WORLD"

Thoughts of what may exist often come to each of us. Most are not acted on so there is never a dream to be lived. Many years ago such a thought became a dream. Three ships left their home port and the land we live in was discovered, a dream was lived. My fellow American, "open your window to see the world"...

By the hands of many the things that make our lives so comfortable were developed and perfected. Just look around you and you will see them everywhere. With comfort comes satisfaction and less of a desire to explore. No one is cursed so that they have no thoughts. Being poor and unknown does not take the ability to think away from you. Mr. Carver overcame and creating peanut butter is his claim to fame. So just "open your window to see the world"...

What you want and desire is known only by you...and getting those things can only be achieved by you. If you want them, it is because you are looking out your window, away from your comfort. Dare to think more comfort is out there waiting on you...dare to take steps to find out if this is true...dare to seek satisfaction beyond the window you find comfort behind. But first, you must "open your window to see the world"...the world that is waiting for you to explore...the world that can bring...you so much more...

June 13, 2009

"PATIENCE VALIDATES ALL THOU ARE"

As the world turns the universe grows older...as your days are lived your years of existence add up...and as you acquire knowledge your wisdom is increased. All things happen for a reason...in order and...in due time...

Time is the driving force that affects all...and success is the measuring stick by which we are all judged. Character is the one trait that all cannot hide... and patience is a key character trait that most don't understand. Yet "patience validates all thou are"...

A race is not won by one...lacking the patience to train. A step is not taken by a child that...lacks patience to first crawl. A book is not read by one... lacking the patience to read each word. Life is not lived by one...lacking the patience to first survive. "Patience validates all thou are" so have patience... and become the best you can be...

You see patience is simply giving a plan...time to develop or giving a theory...time to be thought through. It is giving a hug time...to earn a kiss or giving an outing time...to be an adventure. It is giving yourself time to mature...giving your thoughts time to develop your character. Patience is giving a friend...time to become a lover and then giving a lover...time to become a soul mate. Patience isn't wasting time, "patience validates all thou are"...and can become...

January 10, 2009

"PLANTING GREENER PASTURES, CLIMBING HIGHER MOUNTAINS"

For many just existing is a great challenge for decisions they made yesterday did not make today a better day, or their dreams for tomorrow were not dreams of reality but just dreams without a way to be realized. That is why I am "planting greener pastures, climbing higher mountains"...

Life is lived with others seeking to live also. We all grow, eat, breeze, learn and hopefully teach day after day. We do this with the help of others, some of which passed many yesterdays ago. Was it not for those who understood the need to be "planting greener pastures, climbing higher mountains" where would we be today...

Plan a life of victory and a victory you can achieve. Learn to live with others and others can live with you. Learn what is there to be learned and you can teach it on tomorrow. Visualize a better you for tomorrow and you can be better when tomorrow comes. Satisfy not thou self in today's accomplishments for tomorrow they will be historical facts and no help for you tomorrow...

Why look for greener pastures when you can make your pasture greener and a reflection of you. Climbing a mountain that many are already standing on, leaves you little space to stand, for it grows more crowded day by day. Make your own mountain to climb and make it hard for others to find...

I am happiest only when I am "planting greener pastures, climbing higher mountains". So if you want to impress me or be special in my life...do it by showing me that you understand the need...to be "planting greener pastures, climbing higher mountains". You know you got it right...when standing on your mountain you see others...trying to get into your greener pastures below...

September 21, 2008

"REALITY REALIGNS YOU"

There is no substitute for dreaming, for by dreaming goals are created for you to achieve, living becomes life and life becomes enjoyable...

When lying is seen as the way to get relief from some known situations, you cease living enjoyably. You now are living to be discovered, to be corrected. So at those times when life threatens your dreams, know that "reality realigns you"...

In reality there is the comfort of truth and the peace that only a clean conscience can bring you. There is also the hope which comes from having faith in others and the pride that others know your strengths. Yes it is true that "reality realigns you"...

Being real with yourself and others keeps you from attempting that which you cannot achieve...promising that you cannot deliver...giving that you don't posses...wanting that you cannot obtain and...living a life in which so much is not realistic. When "reality realigns you" let it be a lesson learned...a blessing from God and...the beginning of living your perfect dream. You will have a life full of joy...and God's promise of eternity...

September 20, 2008

"SECRETS YOU DON'T TELL"

Living is a continuous journey for us all. How one chooses to live is all on them. Though many factors may affect how one does live, often it is "secrets you don't tell" that have clouded one's vision of living to affect how one lives...

"Secrets you don't tell" are always on one's mind. Pulling the focus away from one's thought processes, disrupting the reasoning of one's conscience and justifying the actions one takes. Yes, the "secrets you don't tell" sometimes make living pure hell...

Just be sure you have a well grounded reference point to guide you through life. Have faith that God will help you no matter what. Trust that those closest to you will understand and love you anyway. Find joy in how the rest of your secrets inspire you and others too. Then the "secrets you don't tell" will be secrets...that don't matter because of the rest of what you do...

May 31, 2010

"STEP OUTSIDE TO DISCOVER YOU"

The baby bird hatched in the nest started the journey into life by breaking the shell that had always protected it so well. Born not able to fly or feed itself, mama bird does all of that. Time passes and the baby chick grows. Then one day mama pushes it out the nest. Cruel you may consider this to be...but the mama bird is just saying "step outside to discover you" fly my chick and learn to live independently...

I stand in the forest for I love the sights, the sounds and the natural world I am in. One tree looks like the next, just as the flowers or grass do. All the creatures living here call it home. I am just visiting and enjoying what God has created. In here I only see that which is around me. I know I cannot see the forest...for I am in the midst of the trees. Sometimes you have to "step outside to discover you" and you will...see the forest you truly are beyond the trees ...

The mind likes what is normal because it knows it well. Likewise, the heart is comfortable with...feeling the same old way. One's character pleases one's self just fine...so that is why you must "step outside to discover you". Maybe you will find the you...that others feel you can be...the new you others want to know. The you that you know is there...in that forest...out there beyond the trees...just out of sight until...you "step outside to discover you"...

August 2, 2008

"STOP"

Business, just like life requires one to seek a path to succeed. In many ways we all try to do that. There is no easy way to accomplish this. Please understand it takes a plan and wit...

Start by studying so you know what it takes then find the best way do just that. Create a strategy so you have a plan for the path is long and difficult my man. Seek an alliance for you can't do it alone...

Talk through your plan with only those you trust knowing a team is only good if all understand and want to follow the plan. Together, yes we can win and overcome the difficulties to make it a successful endeavor...

Organizing yourself first, you must do for how can you lead others if they can't see that you know the way. Open up to let others see exactly what you are about. Yes, show them the true you especially your heart...

People are your only weapons in this war. The perfect performance is achieved only if they believe. Provide them with a victory while showing mercy for all. Mostly put God first and let him show you the way. Prepare for tomorrow so your work of today is not in vain...

"Stop" usually means something must change...but it also means more if you allow it to be. Not much is possible if you don't change to live by this lesson to gain wealth and fame...

December 21, 2008

"TEARS JUST CLEANSE YOUR JOY"

I remember following along as the older Christian folks sang one of the Old 100's. I also remember my thoughts back then. Although I listened and tried to understand in my mind I could not duplicate how I felt they were feeling. I asked why they cried so much so the old ones would just smile and say "tears just cleanse your joy"...

A mother watches as child after child walks across that stage, more anxious she grows as each name is called. Soon the tears she can't hold back for she knows her child's special moment is near. I had to know why her tears were different from the rest so I asked her friend. That child almost died at birth and almost died a time or two since, my friend knows "tears just cleanse your joy"...

You see "tears just cleanse your joy" no matter your name or what the situation may be. No, never be ashamed, embarrassed or too upset to cry for you must cry tears of joy to wash sorrows away. Cry to celebrate the great things God does for you. Cry to show you are happy to live another day. Cry to show your loved ones that you care for "tears just cleanse your joy"...

So when you see someone crying...I hope it affects you too. Let them have their moment...as I think they would give to you. You never know when your joy will overcome you so stay ready...for your heart knows "tears just cleanse your joy"...

October 10, 2008

"THAT OLE RIVER KEEPS RISING"

Playing in the yard as a child had challenges which appeared to be too hard to conquer, but we tried and did conquer them. We didn't know or realize how "that ole river keeps rising"...

Going to school and growing up gave us the first true understanding of what there was to learn in life. There were many more challenges like education, friendships, love and even chores and work. We could now see how "that ole river keeps rising"...

Our college days introduced us to so much more. There was responsibility, true love and relationships, personal character and living on our own. We could now feel how "that ole river keeps rising"...

Working for a living introduced a higher level of responsibility that we had not seen. Pressure and unknown challenges...were true life changing opportunities. We faced the need to succeed...to survive and have a good standard of life. Oh, now we are in the middle of life...and "that ole river keeps rising"...

A great spouse and kids are what drives my life now...and although "that ole river keeps rising" I know I am prepared to keep rising...just conquering...what that ole river floats my way...

June 28, 2008

"THE BACKGROUND HIGHLIGHTS THE STARS"

I run fast to reach the end zone, eluding would be tacklers is the only way to get there. I score to hear the crowd cheering and have my teammates congratulate me. The coaches give their approval while asking for more of the same. Yet I am not satisfied...until I make contact with my family to see that they are pleased too. For they define me and complete the person you praise. "The background highlights the stars" that we often admire...

These words you read are a reflection of me. You may like or hate them...that my friend is a reflection of thee. If they are printed in white font on white paper they will be there...yet you will not see them. Only when "the background highlights the stars" will you be able to see my reflection...and compare it to the reflection of thee...

When you are affected by all that you encounter...give yourself a moment to focus on the background too. It is then that what you encounter will be more visible to you. Be it a person, book or image...it takes the right background to make it sparkle...like the stars against the darkness of space. "The background highlights the stars" so that you know the right ones...to wish upon, dream about or remember forevermore...

May 30, 2010

"THE LUXURY OF LIFE"

If you are blessed to truly understand life enough to define it...if your definition of life is definable by other too...and if you know how to benefit from knowing these two things...you know "the luxury of life" so live it well...

Each day of your life you face the entire universe...you view about the same perspective that you viewed yesterday every day. No, you don't see it all...but if you understand "the luxury of life" you can visualize how it changes too...

When you are wake...you have the power to observe...the opportunity to improve...the chance to help and many supporting entities...that you should let know that you appreciate what they mean to you. Being lost in your own life... causes you to not recognize "the luxury of life" so live to become more, not just to survive...

"The luxury of life" is easy to see if you just see beyond thee. It is easy to feel if you open your arms to receive hope. It is easy to taste if you have no hatefulness on the tip of your tongue. It is easy to smell if your nose is not filled with the scent of greed and deceit. Oh, how easy it is to touch...if your heart is filled with love and joy. "The luxury of life" is your buried treasure within...a treasure that can only be discovered if you...define it to be a luxury for all to see...

January 24, 2010

"THE PATH TO GREATNESS IS A LONELY ADVENTURE"

Why are there so many that follow and so few that lead? Most of us think that we know the answer. We think that leadership is for the strongest or most knowledgeable. We feel inspired by their deeds and take comfort in following as they lead. Just take a moment to consider the whole picture. There you will realize that "the path to greatness is a lonely adventure" that many of us should consider living too...

Those that follow, still have to decide their path in life for you must decide to follow the leader. You have to evaluate your readiness to walk the path that is before you, the footprints of one that leads the way. You have to be faithful to follow and hope that you decided wisely. You have to commit to being one that follows and helps the others like you. In your times of sorrow, as you watch others lose their way, maybe you will begin to see that "the path to greatness is a lonely adventure", an adventure that God created for you...

Many can start the journey in hopes of enduring to the end. Many can visualize the process of how to win. Many can tell you just how to overcome to become victorious. Many can walk, when there is no burden to bear. Many can challenge for the leading position, yet they lack the true will to be the leader they truly wish to be. "The path to greatness is a lonely adventure" so how good of a leader do you want to be...

If you can hide the tracks of your tears, while others weep and whine. If you can step above the fear, while other cry for a hero. If you can travel one more mile, while others fail to move on. If you can endure the loneliness, as you journey on all by yourself. Then you become the leader for you truly know that "the path to greatness is a lonely adventure"...yet you make it, for those needing hope that they too can achieve more...

August 27, 2011

"THE SUN MUST SET TO ENJOY ANOTHER SUNRISE"

Each motion requires a resistance to occur. So each time that your emotions change, something must happen for you to have a different emotional feeling. You see "the sun must set to enjoy another sunrise" that will truly affect how your emotions flow...

If your life was only lived joyously, soon you would not know that it is joy that you are feeling. Accept despair and discomfort as a sunset for "the sun must set to enjoy another sunrise" that gives you hope of having more joyous memories to share...

When you love, understand that so many factors continuously affect how you accept and give love. In trying times when you are feeling hurt or love seems to be slipping away, know that it takes some cloudiness to create a beautiful sunset. Always remember that "the sun must set to enjoy another sunrise" and a little cloudiness makes the sunrise more special too...

November 7, 2010

"THE STORM IS NATURE'S SONG OF TRIUMPH"

The clouds are upon me now, making it dark and gloomy...like the cellar below. Clouds oh clouds, how did you get here and from where did you come. You make no sound yet you are here...the canvas over nature's musical stage...

Oh, how I can feel your strength Mr. Wind. That strength which rearranges the world as nature prepares to play its song. Mr. Wind you started the song with whispering notes...then those whispering notes were transformed into howling notes. I just have to listen as nature plays notes that can never be duplicated...

Now comes the exciting blows as the sword of nature strikes time...and time again. Nothing is strong enough to survive those mighty blows...most just explode as nature's power is displayed. Lightning oh lightning...we applaud how you put on such a magnificent lighting show...

What is a mighty warrior if at the end of a victory...it does not shout to let others know it has won? The booming thunder reverberates like...a magnificent drum while at the same time...it is warning of where the battling is being done. Nature ole nature...I think you have already won the battle...for we no longer see the mighty sun...

"The storm is nature's song of triumph" for her victory...over the Universal Warriors as they keep trying to get her out of balance. They try to rip her armor apart and dislodge her sword, lightning from her hands. They try to silence the magnificent booming drum beat...but the thunder still roars...

The storm is nature's song of victory to let us know...we are safe behind her armor...and in her loving arms. When the storm is raging there is no need to fear...just respect and protect her when you can. Live your life in comfort and when nature wins a great victory...show some respect for her strengths...for her never ending battle...she fights for us. "The storm is nature's song of triumph" sit silently...as she plays...

October 16, 2008

"THE WEARY HUNTER MUST HUNT TO SURVIVE"

The seasons are not kind to all. Each of God's creatures must live through the tough times just to survive, to see better times. In the worst of times they all grow weary. The survivors know that even 'the weary hunter must hunt to survive" the worst of times...

Seldom is a championship not a contested one for the competition is never very less inspired than the champion. Often the champion finds that the difference between a loss and a win is the result of the hunter like instincts within. When pushed to the limit of his abilities, the champion must find more courage and the will to win. In those times he knows that "the weary hunter must hunt to survive" the pressure and drive of the competitors...

The American dream is there on display for all to know and hope to achieve. It is like the prey that knows the hunter is near and attempting to make the kill. It will not set still and be easily taken...for it too seeks to survive forevermore. Oh Dreamer, just be aware of your abilities and skills...make a plan that allows your weary body to have a chance. Study your prey hoping your weary state... does not spoil your chances. Conquer your fears...remove the doubt that may be there. Have faith in you...for you have survived thus far. Be the hunter that certainly knows...that "the weary hunter must hunt to survive"...to dream then feast on the belief of those dreams...

January 30, 2010

"THE WIND SINGS ITS SONG"

If only you would sit still and be quiet would you be able to know that "the wind sings its song". A song no man could have written or composed...and a song that no man can sing. So listen...listen so you can live...

You could also learn so much about nature, mother earth and the world...if you can learn to hear and interpret the meaning that...the wind brings to your senses. "The wind sings its song" that most do not understand...so the song is seldom appreciated...and the warning goes unknown...

When "the wind sings its song" I try to understand and interpret it all. I process where it is coming from...to know where it is going. I then can feel how fierce it is...by how it attacks my skin. I truly hope you know too...that those are its only warning signs. My other senses can smell what it brings to me. Like the promise of rain or an approaching dust storm. If your senses are keen enough it even warns...that danger may be near...

No the wind is not just a nuisance or welcomed relief when the temperature is too hot. "The wind sings its song" for all of us to hear. Listen closely and hear its song my brother and...then go teach others to hear it too. For when "the wind sings its song", nature is rebalancing herself. Be it a small or large rebalance, it will affect you man...so listen to how the wind sings...and live to sing your song...

August 31, 2008

"THEIR EMPTY PROMISES ARE NOW OUR DREAM"

Under the covers someone has hope because a candle lights the darkness as children are learning. Oh how those first words were cherished by the children. Yes, they were first spoken then they were learned. Back in the Motherland our hearts loved, we trusted others, a mistake our forefathers came to know for "their empty promises are now our dream"...

In their fancy suits, they called our names saying trust us to deliver you freedom. We also promise you a well lived life. Carpet Baggers they became known as and little did we receive. Later we realized that "their empty promises are now our dream"...

Many years passed and we received so many more promises...and far too few chances to become more. We fought at first with violence till Martin showed us the way. His life was taken in hope of shattering his dream, stealing what we had gained. The evil ones in America "their empty promises are now our dream"...

The modern politicians and country leaders make a big show of caring by allowing us to progress while they progress more. Still we progressed from the strength of our bodies, from the sweat of our brows because "their empty promises are now our dream"...

Be it dreams of equality or our chances to leave our plights behind us...our progress has always been made somewhat under cover...but at last a victory of significance has been won. Our first Black President is now a reality. Truly, "their empty promises are now our dream". So now that we are living the dreams of our brothers of the past...we can dream for so much more...

November 06, 2008

"THIS CHAMPIONSHIP IS MINE"

As the lion would stalk its prey I have studied those which challenge me. They will not fall easily I know. More importantly to me, I know "this championship is mine" because I have earned it...

As the great hunter readies to make the shot, I too ready myself to race. I already know what it takes and I know I have it. I need only to conquer my fears to make me the winner. I fear not the challengers for I know "this championship is mine" because I put in the training time...

Today I asked God to be with me so now I feel His presence. I feel the wind aiding my thin frame against the bigger challengers. I feel the strength in my legs for nature nourishes my body. I feel the joy in my soul for I compete with hope and faith. The time is near now and there is no fear for I know "this championship is mine" I need only to race...

My last thought as the timer fires the gun is...Lord I am ready...I know my task ...I feel your presence...and I am comforted in knowing you are with me this day. "This championship is mine" because you made it to be...just as you made me to be the champion that I am...

July 13, 2008

"THIS LIGHT KEEPS ON SHINING"

Time is not man's enemy as so many think it is. It is our provider, our only constant in life. Man need only to respect time and utilize it well...

Time keeps on passing, leaving yesterday to be remembered, today to be lived and tomorrow to be dreamed. Time, the never ending drumbeat of which all things are measured and hopefully enjoyed...

Time is the light that leads us day by day. It sets the pace of our hearts, our motions and even our thoughts. This light shines in our lives from the womb to the tomb...

Time ole time please set the tempo of my heartbeat. Keep me thinking to keep pace with the world. Keep my thoughts focused on living to appreciate my yesterday, enjoy my today and faithfully look forward to tomorrow...

"This light keeps on shining" in me...for others to see and know I respect time. "This light keeps on shining" so time keeps pace with the rest of God's creations...that are all measured by time. Time is the peaceful constant and time is my friend...that always light up my life. Because of time, "this light keeps on shining" within...as well as all around me...

August 23, 2008

"THIS POWER WITHIN YOU"

We all have old baggage that resides in the subconscious. A bad memory is like a lion stalking prey. Silently it waits, undetected because it is masked by the fond memories that you want to relive. It creeps into your dream for it wants to be relived. The nightmare comes without warning and your joy is the target that it never misses. "This power within you" reacts just right and confines that bad memory in the deepest, darkest chamber of your mind...

On yesterday you feared viewing your image in the mirror for there were times when that image was not you. You saw a broken spirit, a beaten and battered soul. You saw the scars of a hateful hand. You saw searching eyes, desperately seeking hope and love. You saw someone...you knew was not you. "This power within you", faith, calmed you while showering you with kindness and joy. Now the image in the mirror is alive once more...

One can beat and abuse you like a fierce hurricane does the shore, but no storm last forever. You kept praying for sunshine and looking for the rainbow to follow. Then "this power within you" led you to that golden treasure chest and you recovered all that you had lost. Hope, love, joy and happiness now reside with faith and "this power within you" helps you grow stronger and more joyous every day. Now you have no fear of viewing...your image in the mirror...

November 27, 2011

"TIME"

In time, the world will appear to not turn, yet your heart will race to prove you belong where you are...

In a day, your tomorrow will become a guiding beacon of how each of your tomorrows should be...

For the moment, your memories of yesterday will have to capture your imagination, yet allow you to dream of the greatest desires of your heart...

Today, you must live between yesterday's greatest memories and tomorrow's dreams...

In your dreams, you become the desire of others and only need to desire that same dream for it to be you, your tomorrow and all of your tomorrows to come...

September 23, 2011

"TRAVELING IN THE RIGHT DIRECTION"

Every road was once just the easiest path from one place to another place... the path became more used and eventually... became the road you see. Maybe it was an insect seeking a food source that blazed it first...then later, those preying on those insects made the path more important. That path was visible enough and it became important for man to travel it...probably in such of prey...but hopefully seeking a dream as well. Till then, there were no rules on that path and "traveling in the right direction" was not an issue...

139

Man was created by God and given a mission to accomplish. That mission had rules that man had to live by. Man is inquisitive by nature and started to explore so he chose a road to travel, breaking rules along the way. As the story is told the rules became many, just to keep man "traveling in the right direction"...

Many roads we travel today are well traveled...crowded and full of pitfalls of despair. "Traveling in the right direction" is much more complicated now...yet just as easy to do as when the insects traveled the same paths so long ago. Be like the insects...learn to take a different path or use reverse to rescue you or get you "traveling in the right direction". You must be a survivor...adding value to your life and the lives of others. Please understand that by traveling with God you are always "traveling in the right Direction"...

August 3, 2008

"TREASURES ARE DISCOVERED WHEN YOU DREAM"

I am not sure how your world is formed in your mind and I cannot clearly explain mine to you. Mine is still like a mystery to me even though I live in it every day. In those times when the mystery seems to be trying to overtake the sensible me, I remind myself that "treasures are discovered when you dream"...

Life is not always what you plan and definitely is not always all that you dream of. Some let this cause them to seek shelter in the shadows of their mind and they lose sight of life itself. Others go beyond and seek shelter in vices which alter their state of being in hopes of finding that perfect dream to shock them back to reality and away from the nightmare they now live in. Someone should remind them that "treasures are discovered when you dream" and then, you can live again...

Locked within me, there is energy that my mind does not know how to command. There is love that no soul can know without my soul revealing the love that it posses. There is passion that is waiting to rush to thee. Thee that proves deserving of the passion within me. There is eternity behind these eyes of mine, just waiting for that right partner that will walk that far with me. Yes "treasures are discovered when you dream" of how wonderful you can make your life become...

August 26, 2010

"TREE TOPS THE SUN NEEDS TO REACH ME"

Are you down on your luck, lost in a storm of despair or wishing not for a miracle...but just to survive? When the place you are in is dark and gloomy just say "tree tops the sun needs to reach me"...please give me a chance to live...

Lord, I need you to cover me with a blanket of hope....give for me a pillow, a mound of faith. Now close my eyes and comfort me with joyous thoughts. Oh Lord, help them understand why I cry "tree tops the sun needs to reach me" for...I must be like you someday...

Those which are not experiencing that which I am just do not understand. You see many of the things that they do keep me in this despair. Competition and greed blinds most of them...so much so that they don't even know that they become like tree tops to...those not strong enough to match what they do. Tree tops block the sunlight from the plants below, diminishing their chance to grow strong and tall. I know how it is to be one of those plants so grant my plea "tree tops the sun needs to reach me" before it is too late...

So when you look at others around you, including me, understand how your strength and leafy branches could affect me. Then trim the unnecessary leaves and branches because "tree tops the sun needs to reach me". I just want to grow toward the heavens...for one day you will not be there. Then it will be me that protects those below with the leaves and branches...that you allowed me to grow...

September 29, 2008

"TYING TIES AND FISHING"

In one's development years there is a lot to learn. It has been suggested that there is little to be learned from "tying ties and fishing". I don't agree so listen to the lessons about living that I know you can learn...

Caring is so important that no one can grow within without a caring soul. When you tie a tie you show you care enough to look your best...to make an effort to impress. When you fish you care enough to learn...and be patient even dedicated to the task. There are laws and techniques you must follow to be a successful fisherman...isn't life the same? Practice "tying ties and fishing" for they are great examples of how...to grow during your lifetime...

Skills are a must in all that we do. Without dedication and determination you will not possess the skills you need to get through life. "Tying ties and fishing" develops your skills...just as classes and practice does. Who wants to step out with a jacked up tie or...one that don't match the attire? Who goes fishing without expecting to make a catch? See there is hope and faith in your every cast... and each cast improves your skills. Life is the same way, for each challenge requires you to give your best to achieve success. Once you have acquired skills at one thing...you know how to acquire skills for other things you must know to succeed. I'm practicing "tying ties and fishing" as I face each challenging day...

I learned to tie ties and fish at a young age and both brought excitement to my life. Each challenged me to become more perfect...and taught me that knowing how does not always mean you will be successful. You have to perform almost flawlessly...to honestly declare you did your best...

"Tying ties and fishing" are symbolic with working and having fun. Between the two extremes is where the real you...struggle to stay balanced. Learn to care, hope and have faith...while being determined and dedicated to what you know is right. Then imagine you are "tying ties and fishing" to understand...just how simple life can be lived...using those skills...

January 16, 2010

"UNDERSTANDING IS THE KEY TO EVERYTHING YOU DO"

Most do not think about understanding very often because most of what we do is just our daily routine. Our minds are programmed to do most of what we must do. So I want to remind you that "understanding is the key to everything you do" even opening your eyes each morning that you wake...

Your mind is the greatest computer that you will every use. It controls all you are, even the twitching of your toes. It is capable of keeping you alive but it requires that you nourish it and feed it information that it does not know. "Understanding is the key to everything you do" so always thirst for knowledge...to make you understand more than you did before...

We prepared for meetings...to understand how to communicate and contribute. We rehearse our scenes or songs...for we understand the audience expects our best. We search our souls for those right words to say...for we know how much our loved ones mean to us. We take care of our bodies...for we understand that if we don't we cannot live. Give these thoughts a moment to sink in and you will know forever that "understanding is the key to everything we do"... including having others know the true person you have grown to be...

March 6, 2011

142

"UNTIL THE RAIN STOPS"

Hold on to the memories that make you feel great...how long, "until the rain stops"...

Find peace in the memories that make you feel safe...how long, "until the rain stops"...

Seek guidance from those that you trust in most...how long, "until the rain stops"...

Listen to the greatest gift of God, nature itself...how long, "until the rain stops"...

Life is not always fair and many others will affect you in ways that you cannot control. The rain is symbolic of the darkest days of your life...when your thoughts are not right and you are too upset to take action. So wait to act... until you are better able to succeed...how long, "until the rain stops"...

In times of peace be thankful...but in times of trouble be faithful. In times of happiness share tears of joy...and in times when you know not what to do, wait...how long, "until the rain stops"...

June 18, 2008

"VALIDATE SOMEONE'S GREATNESS, BE GREATER"

As he waited across the net, his opponent stood so confident and determined to win. He knew of the greatness of those before him and understood how his own performance would matter to those that followed. He was different from the rest just because of the color of his skin. Though many waited for him to falter, he just continued to win. Win the matches and win the hearts of those that knew of his journey. To those that play tennis today, "validate someone's greatness, be greater" than Arthur Ash...

On a farm he learned so much of what he knew. His family taught him to value life and the farm taught him the laws of nature. So young and so frightened he must have been...to leave home in search of greater knowledge. For coupled with wisdom...it would give him a chance to realize a dream. Most of us love his creation, including modern day scientists. Be it creamy or crunchy, let it give you energy to..."validate someone's greatness, be greater" than George Washington Carver and create something special too...

Who do you look up to...who drives you to achieve...who reminds you to be great? Who is there to help you if you falter...who celebrates your victories with you? It matters not who, it only matters that...there is someone. "Validate someone's greatness, be greater" than that someone...at what you chose to do...

December 25, 2009

"WE ARE ALL RICH WHEN WE KNOW WHAT TO TREASURE"

My child greets me with a big smile with excitement in those eyes and a loving kiss on the cheek. My God allows my eyes to open each morning and my senses I still have. I have comfort and security for those I love and me...

My job, yes I have one. My education I worked hard to acquire but my wisdom is a testament of how I have lived. My pet, be it swimming, perching, wagging a tail or purring it is always wanting my touch. My car starts to carry me where I want to go. The planes I have been on all took off and landed safely. My old legs and feet that move to my heart beat have never failed me yet...

When you know the trials and tribulations God has delivered you from and know that your leaps of faith have brought you through. If you understand the importance of love and have felt the joyousness inside when your hope has allowed you to achieve. Tell me what else do you need? "We are all rich when we know what to treasure" and...know to appreciate what means the most to us...

Look around you and try understanding what you see. Process it in your mind to consciously determine what you have versus what you need. The wealthy have their purpose just as you; however, you are wealthier than they when...you understand "we are all rich when we know what to treasure"...

September 21, 2008

"WE GET A NEW BEGINNING EVERYDAY"

As each day unfolds we are faced with living and making decisions which will affect who we are and what others think of us. There are no perfect days...for none of us are perfect in any way. We must trust in ourselves first...to gain the trust of others and trust them the same. You can live life in a way that is uplifting ...if you know that "we get a new beginning everyday"...

The right answer is sometimes acquired...only after you eliminate the wrong answers. The picture you paint...is often not the image you imagined with the first stroke on the canvas. The journey that you remember fondly...was not the adventure that you set out to live. No, today's reality...was not how you dreamed today to be. "We get a new beginning everyday" so learn from your living and get better everyday...

What is special...we treasure and protect. Hopefully love, faith, compassion and the joy of knowing God in your heart.. are treasures you have stored in your chest. Live to grow stronger and better each day...for it fill your chest with more of these treasures. Then each night go to sleep...thinking of your positive memories of today and yesterday. This will allow you to dream positively...for you know that "we get a new beginning everyday"...

December, 26 2010

"WEEP NOT, ENJOY"

All will never be just as you want it to be but "weep not, enjoy" that which is...

When I am not there the tears will not change a thing "weep not, enjoy" your loving memories of being with me...

When the sun sets on the horizon and that beautiful sunset is gone forevermore "weep not, enjoy" just save it as a memory and relive it for years to come...

When your dreams appear to never be coming true and it disappoints you greatly "weep not, enjoy" the positive things that have occurred in your life for that will allow your dreams to grow into a dream that comes true...

When they close that door to never show my face again "weep not, enjoy" knowing that...I have joy in Heaven and will be watching over you forevermore. "Weep not, enjoy" life as it is...and it will allow you to be joyous forevermore...

October 17, 2007

"WHAT ARE YOU WILLING TO GIVE YOUR LIFE"

That which is normal we just expect to stay the same. That which annoys us we want it to just go away. That which we truly enjoy, we value as a treasure. The life we are living we hope becomes the life we want to live. My question to you "what are you willing to give your life"...

Are you willing to give your life a chance, a chance to develop by trying to better yourself...a chance to find peace by creating peace within you...peace that others want to be a part of too. A chance to love comes to you...only when you are loveable too and when loving you is...what makes another's dream come true. A chance to give, by accepting God's gift to you...and using it positively...by giving too. A chance to lead by first following...those which know the way...so then some day you will not only know the way...you can make a better way...

"What are you willing to give your life" the only life you get to live. Will you give it eternity...by making it a life that others keep alive in their memories of you? Will you give it all that you have to give...so the day does not come that you curse yourself? Will you find yourself crying in defeat...for you didn't give your best? Will you find yourself emerged in hopeless loneliness...for not giving in to love because of...your fear of losing yourself...

Ask yourself these questions then make a plan...so you will be able to answer forevermore "what are you willing to give your life"...

October 18, 2008

"WHAT GOOD IS TOMORROW"

We should always be able to have fond memories of yesterday and we should always keep in mind today... how important yesterday is to who we are today. For "what good is tomorrow" to those...that prepared not for tomorrow on yesterday...

Life is full of surprises for us all...for all of us face the unknowns of tomorrow. Now man can predict or plan for tomorrow...but never truly know the outcome until tomorrow becomes today. "What good is tomorrow" if you do not know...if you achieved your dreams of yesterday? How can you then... dream of tomorrow...

"What good is tomorrow" if your life today is meaningless...lived in despair or made complicated by self imposed problems...if you are lacking hope, missing the love of others or...if there is the absence of believing in God? Can you have hope...that tomorrow will come...

What good is tomorrow" if you are not, excited about waking to start your day...driven to achieve or live your dreams or...if you can't wait to be with those you love. "What good is tomorrow" if you cannot face yourself...because you failed yourself...yesterday...

July 26, 2008

"WHEN THE RIVER MEETS THE MOUNTAINS"

A troubled Life is not too hard to have for it is easy to do nothing and it is easier to not learn. It is easy to ignore nature's magnificent power so find that point in your life where you know "when the river meets the mountains"...

Good relationships are not a given, you must want to do what makes a relationship and then do more to make that relationship a good relationship. Search your thoughts and even your soul so "when the river meets the mountains" you are able to find your way to the ocean...

The ocean is a constant as nature meant it to be for it is the heavenly body of water that all waters want to join. Water flows from the mountains to the ocean just as we live from the cradle to the grave. If you want to know where you are, you must know "when the river meets the mountains" to know your path to eternity...

Back track your life to that point in time when you became aware of life and how you must live your life. That is "when the river meets the mountains", the point in which you started living on your own. Every great person started just the same, like that trickle of water seeping out of a rock in the mountain. Find your way to the stream then to the creek. Now rest a while in the lake of understanding. Then avoid the pitfalls which will keep you damned up or divert you to a path which will certainly delay your journey. Spill over into a river then flow past the sandy shores of despair. Here allow a joyous life to grow within you to provide other creatures of nature a better way to live...

Keep building up momentum for the shallows are ahead. You will be driven by the faithless ones into rocks of pain and thrown from your comfort zone, your loving ways. Now by God's will you will fall back into the river of life and journey on in search of eternity...

147

Stay focused on the journey along the path to eternity by avoiding all the setbacks along the way. Then eventually you will reach the ocean, that heavenly body on earth. So if you want to know how you got here it is as simple as traveling back to your beginning, to "when the river meets the mountains" when your journey to eternity became the mission of your life …

October 05, 2008

"WHEN TOMORROW BECOMES YESTERDAY"

Silence is the beginning and the end of one's life, for one is all alone till birth and it is the same when God calls one home. You must write your script of life and live it at the same time, making changes as life dictates the stage upon which you must act. "When tomorrow becomes yesterday" there will be no Oscar, there will only be another day to live...

Tomorrow is unknown and you can only plan for and dream of how you want it to be. Life continues to change with every breath that you take so your tomorrow will change all that you are. Continue to dream of tomorrow so "when tomorrow becomes yesterday" you can continue to dream of tomorrow...

Today you are living and your dreams of tomorrow will be contingent on how you lived today. Waste not a single moment for you know from yesterday that you won't get to live that moment again. "When tomorrow becomes yesterday" your today will still be between them like a bridge between what you cherish and that which you dream of...

Your yesterday is never truly gone for it is forever with you. Most of it you forget, for it has little value today and you must make room in your heart for all of your dreams. Cherish the greatest moments of yesterday for it will strengthen you today and fuel your soul with desires of what you want tomorrow to be. Live life as a continuous dream of tomorrow for it will allow you to love living today while cherishing the best of your yesterdays. Then "when tomorrow becomes yesterday" your soul will have a greater desire of living tomorrow over and over again...

September 18, 2010

"WHILE THE SKY TURNS BLUE"

Listen to the sound of power...nature's thundering symphony displayed on her stage earth...which is so vivid during the lightning flashes. Her fierce winds, oh how they howl at the height of the storm. Just take a moment to reflect..."while the sky turns blue"...

In you there are similar storms. Some are hardly noticeable while others are quite fierce. The constant is one's conscience and the character it gives you. While the storms are raging inside...just keep focused on your dreams and your mission in life. This is only possible...if you have a reference point that guides you...

Hold firmly to your values while clinging to your hope...then just wrap the rope of faith around you...trusting God always. Do this, "while the sky turns blue" and...you will always be able to enjoy the music that you play ...

"While the sky turns blue"...others will be looking at you. Some wait for their chance to get you...then others are there if you appear to be falling. Some cannot bear to watch you fight...while others admire your might. No treasures on earth can help you through...for it is all up to you...to be your best "while the sky turns blue"...

November 1, 2008

"WHO DO YOU DREAM FOR"

Alone at night or in a quiet place during the day...one is left with one's own thoughts...thoughts of living and being who you are...thoughts of peace... thoughts of tomorrow and...thoughts that inspire you to dream one more dream...

When all is not as you would like it to be...you have to be more like you want to be...if not, you will become less than you want to be...by settling for what is. You can only be what you want to be...if you dream of being just that. So "who do you dream for"...do you really know...

If you only dream for you...your life will be empty for others will not be there. When I ask myself "who do you dream for" many thoughts come to mind. That is why I dream of me...being significant to others. I dream of tomorrow being better...for what I did today was significant. I dream of a peaceful world...for our leaders learned yesterday why...there was no peace. I dream and so do you...so hopefully you will know when asked..."who do you dream for"...

January 20, 2009

"YOU MUST APPRECIATE TO RELATE"

Your attire is an important part of you for shoes protect your feet, undergarments are for comfort, outer wear is to cover and protect, and a hat protects or just highlights it all. Each has a purpose and we all have our own preferences so when you checkout another's attire "you must appreciate to relate" to how they feel...

Likewise, a car has its purpose just as a bike or a toy. We choose the ones we like or want, but we always choose the ones necessary to satisfy a need. They are seldom perfect for the cause, but they always suffice. Learn that "you must appreciate to relate" to the importance of that which you have...

Relationships are more important...so they are more challenging and difficult too. The other person has needs just like you, character and a personality too. Your judgment has to be the check that balances your heart's desires...and your understanding has to be the check that balances your wishful thinking. "You must appreciate to relate" to others in your life...

Feelings come and go...and trust is earned and kept. We cannot control our understanding of others ...but maybe our own. We can learn what is possible... as we know who we are. A man will never be just like a woman...no matter how much you want it to be. We each have a purpose in finding a mate to share life with. You must appreciate the other...before having as a mate. You must work at relating instead of...trying to make the mate the perfect mate for thee. "You must appreciate to relate" then you...can love each other ...hopefully forevermore...

January 31, 2009

"YOUR HEART MUST FUEL YOU A LIFETIME"

You may not understand exactly how it works or how to care for it. You may not know how it knows to change how you feel. You may not know that it is similar to an energy source until you need it to live. "Your heart must fuel you a lifetime" so care for it each and every day...

Any energy source can be depleted if you don't manage your use of it. Use not your heart in a foolish manner for you are just wasting fuel. Fueling temptations or evil endeavors uses double energy, energy you will need some day. Fueling deceit and wrong doing just steals the energy of your soul. Do you not understand that "your heart must fuel you a lifetime" and you have just one life to live...

A heart needs a positive environment to replenish itself. Joy is a key ingredient, so don't let others steal your joy. Peace is the igniter that the heart needs to energize, so don't burden yourself with issues you cannot change. Faith is the regulator which makes sure the heart provides just what your body needs, so let no one or nothing but God affect its setting. Your lifetime is in your control from the cradle to the grave. Knowing "your heart must fuel you for a lifetime", what will you do to make sure it brings you happiness day after day...

September 12, 2010

"YOUR WINGS SUPPORT THE WEIGHT OF YOUR WORLD"

Time keeps passing and issues keep happening, this is just living. Love keeps being something you feel...something you need...and even the one thing you are living for. Happiness is the emotional state that we seek to achieve, not just often, but always. That is how we evaluate how are living...

Peace, oh how it eludes us...and not because we do not try to achieve and live peacefully. There are other things and others that affect how peaceful we live. This too is just living. Faith, now that is for those who do live, believe in themselves, and oh yes, and believe in God almighty. Without faith you are alive...yet you are not living...

Built of love, happiness, peace and faith, "your wings support the weight of your world". By making your life worth living during the most trying or worst of times...you are living, to again see the best of times. I hope you know that this is living...

June 22, 2008

FUN ONES

"Laughter is proof that there is some balance in your life"...

"Children have so much fun because their minds are not burdened with the pressure of living"...

"EIGHT SECONDS"

As a young cowboy you quickly learn how to be a man. You work daily for the laws of nature dictate that you do. Life is not all work, we also get to play. Most of all we have competition to showcase our cowboy skills. Bull riding is the toughest of all, for "eight seconds" you try not to fall...

It is not the competition for all for it takes a special person to compete. There are no time outs...and the bulls don't play. They compete and their game plan is to make you fall off. Their only prize is...to horn in on your business. Clowns, oh clowns I need thee because make it or not...I must get off. You make the difference that allows me to live. It is because of you...I can concentrate on my "eight seconds" of fame...

I make the decision to ride. Just a nod of the head...and it is on! It is all about strength and balance...more weight will help you none...for it is mental toughness...that gets you through. The crowd will cheer for you no matter the outcome...for that "eight seconds" ...you are all that matters...

For "eight seconds" the world stands still. No one can help you...only your skills...so all thoughts and focus must be on holding on. I'm matching the bull's moves...with moves of my own...I got a good seat...and I am in my own world. I'm giving it my best...to earn the status of...being the best. It looks violent to many...but there is no greater peace than knowing...you have the bull bested. It is only when the horn sounds ..that you know you were good enough...to make "eight seconds"...

The ride is over and the clowns save my bacon...so my world can again merge... with the world that we all know. I am just a man again...as I hear the crowd cheering. The announcer shouts out the score for all to know; however...most bullriders already know their score. For the score that matters within...is besting the bull...lasting to the end. Man, there is no better feeling for a bullrider than...making "eight seconds" again...

February 1, 2009

"HEY LITTLE LADY"

Hey little lady, what is on your mind? What is going on behind those eyes that we all see...

I read your eyes and expressions and I know something is going on in that mind of yours...because the eyes, they do not lie...

I watch your body language and know you be thinking something. You must not be sure that you want me to know what that is...

I know within me there is something brewing. I do not know if you see it when you are trying to read me...

"Hey little lady" let's sit and talk a while...make each other smile...make this moment last a while. Let's try to discover that...which is now a mystery for me. "Hey Little Lady" will we...love each other forevermore?

October 25, 2007

"I AM A CANDLE"

I am a candle, and I come in many shapes, sizes and colors. I come to you as a gift, even if you buy me yourself.

What, you don't like my scent...how can that be? You don't like my shape... shame on me. Just remember "I am a candle"...I give you light...

When the power is out my size, my shape, and my scent doesn't matter at all. It is my light that warms your heart, for without light darkness comes. Darkness bringing the mysteries of the unseen and a chilly discomfort of the unknown...

Stow me away or give me as a gift. Use me to make that moment special or make your bath seem so much nicer...I don't mind... "I am a candle"...

When you need me or just want to have me light your way...or you just want to enjoy my scent. If you want me to set the mood...just set me where you want me to be. Okay, focus on my wick then strike a match or click your Bic to light my wick. Now, just relax and watch me work...I will flicker till I am just right and then...I will give you light..."I am a candle"...

It is then you should remember...that I'm giving you more than just light... for I basically melt away as you enjoy me...I exist for you, "I am a candle"...light my fire...

October 4, 2008

"IF I COULD NOT SEE"

I feel the breeze on my face and it makes me think so I close my eyes to try feeling that breeze, yes I still feel it. The picture has a frame...

Keeping my eyes closed I seek to know more. That is when I hear the rustling of the leaves...the chirping of birds...and the sounds of the city. Wow, the picture now has images on the canvas...

I need and want a better picture so I focus more. Yes the air smells clean and the baked goods, coffee and perfume...all remind me of the good things in life. The images now have color and details...

Now I know that "if I could not see"...I still can see...for my senses will paint a picture for me. I need only to use them...by understanding and appreciating their importance to me. Yes close your eyes and you too will find...that without your eyes...you too can see...

June 21, 2008

"OH ROCK LET THY HARBOR BE"

Many legends are told about thee, but just how you were formed no man truly knows. So many lost souls are resting on the ocean floor around you. How they got there the books do tell their tales. There are heavenly souls...and souls bound for hell as well. "Oh rock let thy harbor be"...a peaceful resting place for those loss souls...

Years and years ago as the history books tell...people discovered the people that were already here. Many battles raged throughout the years...so thank God we are civilized now. The Rock is culturally enriched...by the people that gather here. Oh rock, my St. Thomas how you welcomed them. "Oh rock let thy harbor be" a beacon of hope for those seeking a better destiny...

Somewhere some years ago you became a place for many to rest and play. Some come for days or weeks...and some for the rest of their lives. You became famous for your relaxing pleasures...so now paradise is how you are explained. Oh rock don't let thy people forget their past. Help them hold on to their great history and heritage. "Oh rock let thy harbor be" paradise...for people like me...

"Oh rock let thy harbor be" a safe haven for people that be "St. Thomians". When they feel that Rock fever coming on...allow them to travel where they desire....while always assuring them...that their rock, St. Thomas, will always be home...

November 23, 2008

Stephen McDonald

"ONE MORE"

Is it just "one more" day, or just another event? Will this day make a difference in your life? Will it be celebrated by you alone or celebrated with those you love. In the end it is just "one more" day in a lifetime...

Your birthday is "one more" day in a lifetime that will always need "one more" day of greatness to be fulfilled. May this birthday find you having "one more" day of greatness to be followed by "one more" day of greatness...from now to eternity...

January 19, 2009

"SOMETIMES I JUST WANT TO PLAY"

I hear the noise and recognize it too, that darn alarm clock again...reminding me that it is time to go to work. I lay there for a few minutes more...because "sometimes I just want to play"...

Driving along the country roads day after day and watching the animals grazing...or the birds flying so freely in the air. I ask myself what are their worries, where is their clock, do they even care? We know it does not work that way for them...and that is why "sometimes I just want to play" just as puppies and kittens do...

Sitting at the desk morning after morning just working away on issues I must address. Some are so wrong and some are just crazy...created by those which are lazy. Looking out the window I see the kids across the way playing in the park. Sadly, I whisper to myself "sometimes I just want to play"...

Looking at the senior citizens that I pass each day...they are moving very slowly on their way...for there is not much of great importance that they do these days. I speak and keep going my way...because I have a busy day...as I remember the sadness in their faces...I think, maybe just maybe, it was envy too. I think somewhere deep inside...they think this each day....Lord I thank you for what I have and that you allow me to live, but "sometimes I just want to play"...

November 27, 2008

"PRECIOUS MEMORIES"

The end of a book usually leaves you hanging or wanting more. I hope this book inspires endless thoughts and dreams for that is how one continues to grow. "Tomorrow will come" and you will be there so it is best to be prepared to live it while planning and being excited about the days to come...

"Who do you dream for", what are your buried treasures, how do you receive and give love, is your faith strong enough to give you hope, are you willing to give of yourself and of that which you possess? "Have you the time" to be there for another, are you hoping that "my life end with a joyous moment", or if you "freeze the moment" or "if time stood still", how you would feel and what would happen to your soul...

Thoughts like this and many more are in this book not only to be read, but also to inspire all to consider a different point of view to understand your own life and the lives of those you love...

Dream, live, inspire, be faithful, caring...and give others hope and your gift of forgiveness...

2011

INDEX

SECTION III: LOVE AND FRIENDSHIP

SECTION IV: INSPIRATION

SECTION V: FUN ONES